I0085687

Building Unity Against Fascism
Classic Marxist Writings

Leon Trotsky, Daniel Guérin, Ted Grant et al

Introduction by Marijke Colle

International Institute for Research and Education, Amsterdam
Resistance Books, London

Both the International Institute for Research and Education and Resistance would be glad to have readers' opinions of this book, its design and translations, and any suggestions you may have for future publications or wider distribution.

Our books are available at special quantity discounts to educational and non-profit organizations, and to bookstores.

To contact us, please write to: Socialist Resistance, PO Box 62732 London SW2 9GQ, Britain, email contact@socialistresistance.org or visit: www.socialistresistance.org

Published by Resistance Books, second printing November 2010
Printed in Britain by Lightning Source
ISBN 978-0-902869-81-3

Introduction and selection © IIRE, October 2010
Published as double issue 42/43 of the Notebooks for Study and Research.
ISSN 0298-7902

The articles in this collection have been transcribed and marked up for the Marxists' Internet Archive, mostly by Einde O'Callaghan but also by Brian Reid, David Walters and Zodiac.

Contents

Introduction
Marijke Colle

Only the hopelessly naive would deny that there are deep reserves of racism in modern society. In the wake of the 2008 credit crunch and the structural crisis of the global capitalist economy, unemployment grows, social security systems are destroyed, more and more people, particularly amongst the young, cannot find an affordable home. In this framework, the easy and demagogical arguments and answers from the fascists and the far right can find a new mass audience. People ask themselves where this renewed success of the extreme right is coming from.

The articles in this book start in the 1920s. Karl Radek and Clara Zetkin show how fascism was created by the severe social crisis of imperialist capitalism. It reflects the impossibility of a "normal" accumulation of capital in the world market. This is tied to very specific factors such as wage levels, labour productivity and access to markets and materials. Fascist seizures of power are intended to *brutally and radically* change the conditions of capitalist exploitation to the advantage of the key groups in monopoly capitalism *and to the disadvantage of the working class.*

From the point of view of the ruling class in a developed society, bourgeois parliamentary democracy is the most efficient way to run the state. Normally, austerity, recession and war give capitalists the higher profits they need. Today's neoliberal parties pledge themselves not only to cuts and austerity, but to racist and anti-democratic policies at home which weaken human rights and bolster NATO's imperialist adventures. James P. Cannon describes McCarthyism as incipient fascism, laying foundations for future attacks. The "war on terror", for example, is also a war against ethnic minorities in the developed countries, and against the right of workers and youth to organise, in order to boost profits. Lurid stories about asylum seekers, mass influxes of foreign workers and, of course, Islamic terrorists on the streets of the world's cities develop a climate in which racist and xenophobic ideas can weaken the ability of working people to defend their rights. At such times, notes Farrell Dobbs, tiny fascist sects can be marginal. While the working class_needs to be ready to defend itself, it is necessary in the early stage to marginalise the fascists politically, and to educate the working class. However, other forms of bourgeois rule are available when austerity measures are not enough, including fascism. These usually involve a greater centralisation of powers for the executive branches of the state, even if this means that parts of the bourgeoisie are forced out of political activity. Yet these options, such as military dictatorships or police states, may not be enough by themselves to atomise and demoralise a working class with millions of members and strong organisational traditions.

Leon Trotsky reveals when and how the ruling class uses a fascist movement to wear down and politically defeat the workers' parties and unions through violence and terror. After it has seized power the fascist movement obliterates working class organisations by banning them and killing or imprisoning key leaders. That leaves the formerly most militant and conscious parts of the working class resigned, deprived of a sense of their collective strength and much less able to formulate a political challenge to the fascist state.

Fascism serves the class interests of the big capitalists and not the unemployed or the small business people. As Trotsky wrote in *What is National Socialism?* (1933): "German fascism, like Italian fascism, raised itself to power on the backs of the petty bourgeoisie, which it turned into a battering ram against the organizations of the working class and the institutions of democracy. But fascism in power is least of all the rule of the petty bourgeoisie. On the contrary, it is the most ruthless dictatorship of monopoly capital."

Daniel Guérin describes how the traditional organisations of the working class are replaced by corporate staff associations, joint worker-employer councils in which the bosses dominate and a massive range of sporting and cultural groups which reinforce the new ruling ideology. All this is cemented with the destruction of dissenting media.

The ruling class is a numerically insignificant part of society and it needs allies in its assault on the organised workers. It finds these allies in sections of society which are affected by economic crises, the collapse of businesses, inflation and unemployment. Universally fascism speaks the language of racism and extreme nationalism, argues that women's place is in the home and perpetrates homophobia.

The fascist movement develops autonomously, slowly building support and articulating in a reactionary way the discontent of those in society with whom the left has failed to connect. However it can only come to power when part of the ruling class decides to back it.

This has to be preceded by a civil war in which the fascists must destroy the workers' movement. Whether or not they succeed depends on how the workers' organisations resist.

Only the united front approach based on the independence of the working class can create the conditions for the success of the antifascist movement. Such a movement must be rooted in, and led by, the working class and its allies in defence of all those in the wider community against fascism and racism.

Antonio Gramsci argues that the working class must defeat capitalism in order to defeat fascism. Fascist organisations capitalise on the disillusionment and deep alienation from the so-called democratic electoral process felt by many working class voters. Ted Grant shows that the working class movement must put the blame squarely on those who pursue profits at the expense of working people. To confront fascism the working class movement needs to not only make a major contribution to the anti-fascist struggles; it must build campaigns and agitation that relate to many of the key issues facing working people, raising demands that undermine the political success of the fascists.

When fascist organisations start to grow, the antifascist movement particularly needs to relate to and develop grassroots organisations in the Black, LGBT and Muslim communities. In particular, the workers' movement needs to raise demands that address and resolve the specific oppression of migrant workers and the black communities, and not only focus on demands aimed at unemployed or unskilled white workers.

We must link the building of a broad united front to the physical defence of streets and communities. If fascist groups start to grow, the working class should be encouraged to develop defence guards in order to protect itself from fascist groups and preserve democratic rights and civil liberties. The same tactic can be used by Black and migrant communities. Ted Grant recounts the successful mass mobilisations against the British fascists in the 1930s, and shows how mass direct action by occupying the streets and picketing their meeting places can prevent fascists from major mobilisations, and from developing their ownership over the streets.

The articles in this collection, therefore, explain the roots of fascism and the tactics needed to delay and defeat its growth. However, the main strength of a collection of classic texts – powerful and overarching comprehensiveness – is also its weakness. Today's generation has to make its own analysis of today's concrete challenges on the basis of the changing balance of forces in society. A subsequent volume to this, due in early 2011, will discuss current topics like state racism; the nature of the day-to-day threat posed by fascism to women, Black people, migrants and to LGBT people; which demands should be raised by today's anti-fascist movement; the populism of modern far right parties and other lessons from the struggle.

To find out more about that book, and about the other studies and research conducted at the IIRE, please visit us at www.iire.org.

Fascism and Communism
Karl Radek

Fascism is no longer a fruit peculiar to Italian soil, but an international phenomenon. Italy is merely the first country where the Fascisti have seized the government, just as Russia is the first country where the proletariat has seized power. But the Fascisti flood is rising in Germany, in Czechoslovakia, and is beginning to stir in the United States, and France, and Austria.[1]

Fascism, as we shall show, is a petty-bourgeois reaction against post-war conditions – a petty-bourgeois reaction that Big Capital is using to fortify itself wherever its rule is threatened. The difference in the condition of the petty bourgeoisie in different countries is much greater than the difference in the condition of the working classes; and the policies of the former therefore vary more than the policies of Labour.

I do not purpose to discuss here the national differences in the Fascist movement, but rather its common features. I shall confine myself to Fascism in central and southern Europe, because up to the present this movement in America and England is still in its infancy.

What common features has Fascism in Italy, Germany, Czechoslovakia, and Austria? It is perfectly obvious of course that Horthy's Government in Hungary pursues the same policy toward Labour that Mussolini's Government pursues in Italy. Both countries are celebrating orgies of reaction, and persecuting Labour. We may say that these persecutions are in Hungary ten times more atrocious than in Italy. And yet, Hungary does not have a Fascist government. An anti-revolutionary government is not necessarily Fascist.

What then distinguishes the Fascisti from the Hungarian White Counter-revolutionists? The Fascist movement is supported by the lower middle classes, while Horthy's Government is supported by the feudal nobility and the capitalists. White governments of the Horthy type, however, do not in the long run serve the ends of a feudal landed aristocracy, but rather of banking and industrial finance. The outcome of Fascist government in modern Europe is the same, because any new

---

[1] Karl Bernhardovich Radek (31 October 1885 - 19 May 1939) was a socialist active in the Polish and German movements before World War I and secretary of the Communist International from 1920 to 1924. This article appeared in Die Rote Fahne, July 29, 1923.

system today must rest upon either the proletariat or high finance; it can no longer rest upon the middle classes.

The difference between a Fascist Government and a White Feudal-Capitalist Government lies in the fact that the latter ' that of Horthy, for instance ' is in the hands of the old ruling classes, who are trying to restore the old conditions, while the Fascist movement, so far as it represents the petty bourgeoisie, brings new men to the front and endeavors to set up a new order that will liberate the common people from the burdens imposed upon them by the war.

What is the ultimate cause of the Fascist movement? The ultimate cause of the Fascist movement is the reduction of great numbers of the middle classes to the condition of the proletariat as an outcome of the war. Disordered public finance, demoralized currency, rising prices, and enormous taxes have pauperized our educated classes, civil servants, army officers, and an important faction of our independent artisans and tradesmen. These people are seeking to save themselves. They are trying to find a new formula for life.

Immediately after the war the Social Democrats and other representatives of the petty bourgeoisie gained control of the government in Germany, Czechoslovakia, Austria, and Italy. The distressed classes we have just mentioned hoped thus to bring about a change in their favor. But such a reform could be won only by a determined struggle with the great capitalists, and the adoption of Socialist measures. The Social Democrats failed, because they feared Big Capital and distrusted the ability of the proletariat. They not only com-promised with their opponents but capitulated to them. This destroyed the faith of both the working people and the middle classes in Socialism itself.

Since the condition of the middle classes grew steadily worse, they were forced to try other methods, and resorted to Fascism, whose motto is: 'Destroy this lying democracy that merely stands for corruption and profiteering and ruins the industrious commons. Let us set up a strong government of bold, vigorous men, competent to run things, who will start our factories going, make our railways pay, give remunerative employment to our starving bourgeoisie, and rescue from ruin the educated classes.'

Capitalists use this Fascist ideology to destroy our impotent democracy. This democracy does not, to be sure, prevent their controlling our economic life, but it is proving a less serviceable tool than they would like...

The petty bourgeoisie in central and southern Europe is nationalist, because it has been systematically trained for many decades to revere nationalism, and because when it compares its present condition with its condition before the war, it believes that it was better off under the old government. The middle classes look back longingly to the good old times, and thus become the victims of the very elements that have brought them to their present pass.

All those who batten on the decay of society – speculators, profiteers, and money leeches of every kind – make the Fascisti their tools to cow Labour and to prevent their employees from raising wages to correspond with the rising cost of living.

These features of Fascism determine the Communists' tactics. Naturally our party must defend the working classes against the Fascisti. Naturally we must defend them by force of arms, for if the Fascisti gain power they will rivet the chains of Capitalism upon us. They will try to recover their own prosperity at the cost of the manual workers. But it does not follow that we must fight Fascism with arms alone; we must employ political measures likewise.

The proletariat must take the initiative in reconstructing the world on a new foundation. This will convince the petty bourgeoisie that a new era is dawning which may save them from their misery. Therefore if we are to conquer Fascism we must win over the petty bourgeoisie. We must convince them that the capitalists and landlords and reactionary army-men are merely using them as tools. Fascism is middle-class Socialism, and we cannot persuade the middle classes to abandon it until we can prove to them that it only makes their condition worse.

Fascism
Clara Zetkin

In Fascism, the proletariat is confronted by an extraordinarily dangerous enemy. Fascism is the concentrated expression of the general offensive undertaken by the world bourgeoisie against the proletariat. Its overthrow is therefore an absolute necessity, nay, it is even a question of the every-day existence and of the bread and butter of every ordinary worker.[2]

On these grounds the whole of the proletariat must concentrate on the fight against Fascism. It will be much easier for us to defeat Fascism if we clearly and distinctly study its nature.

Hitherto there have been extremely vague ideas upon this subject not only among the large masses of the workers, but even among the revolutionary vanguard of the proletariat and the Communists.

Hitherto Fascism has been put on a level with the White Terror of Horthy in Hungary.

Although the methods of both are similar, in essence they are different. The Horthy Terror was established after the victorious, although shortlived, revolution of the proletariat had been suppressed, and was the expression of vengeance of the bourgeoisie.

The ringleaders of the White Terror were a quite small clique of former officers. Fascism, on the contrary, viewed objectively, is not the revenge of the bourgeoisie in retaliation for proletarian aggression against the bourgeoisie, but it is a punishment of the proletariat for failing to carry on the revolution begun in Russia.

The Fascist leaders are not a small and exclusive caste; they extend deeply into wide elements of the population.

We have to overcome Fascism not only militarily, but also politically and ideologically. The reformists even to-day consider Fascism to be nothing else but naked violence, the reaction against the violence begun by the proletariat.

---

[2] Clara Zetkin (née Eißner; 5 July 1857 - 20 June 1933) was an influential socialist German politician and a fighter for women's rights. Until 1917, she was active in the Social Democratic Party of Germany, then she joined the Independent Social Democratic Party of Germany (USPD) and its far-left wing, the Spartacist League; this later became the Communist Party of Germany (KPD), which she represented in the Reichstag during the Weimar Republic from 1920 to 1933. This article appeared in Labour Monthly, August 1923, pp.69-78.

To the reformists the Russian Revolution amounts to the same thing as Mother Eve's biting into the apple in the Garden of Eden.

The reformists trace Fascism back to the Russian Revolution and its consequences. Nothing else was meant by Otto Bauer at the Unity Congress at Hamburg, when he declared that a great share of the blame for Fascism rests on the Communists, who had weakened the force of the proletariat by continual splits. In saying this he entirely ignored the fact that the German Independents had made their split long before the demoralising example was given by the Russian Revolution. Contrary to his own views, Bauer, at Hamburg, had to draw the conclusion that the organised violence of Fascism must be met by forming defence organisations of the proletariat, because no appeal to democracy can avail against direct violence. At any rate, he went on to explain that he did not mean such weapons as insurrection or a general strike which did not always lead to success. What he meant was the co-ordination of parliamentary action with mass action. What was to be the nature of these actions Otto Bauer did not say, but this is the very point of the question. The only weapon recommended by Bauer for the fight against Fascism was the establishment of an International Bureau of Information on world reaction. The distinguishing feature of this new-old International is its faith in the power and permanence of bourgeois domination, and its mistrust and cowardice towards the proletariat as the strongest factor of the world revolution. They are of the opinion that against the invulnerable force of the bourgeoisie the proletariat can do nothing else but act with moderation and refrain from teasing the tiger of the bourgeoisie.

Fascism, with all its forcefulness in the prosecution of its violent deeds, is indeed nothing else but the expression of the disintegration and decay of capitalist economy, and the symptom of the dissolution of the bourgeois State. This is one of its roots. Symptoms of this decay of capitalism were observed even before the war.

The war has shattered capitalist economy to its foundation, resulting not only in the colossal impoverishment of the proletariat, but also in deep misery for the petty bourgeoisie, the small peasantry and the intellectuals. All these elements had been promised that the war would bring about an amelioration of their material conditions. But the very opposite has happened.

Large numbers of the former middle classes have become proletarians, having entirely lost their economic security. Their ranks were joined by large masses of ex-officers, who are now unemployed. It was among these elements that Fascism recruited quite a considerable contingent.

The manner of its composition is also the reason why Fascism in some countries is of an outspoken, monarchist character.

The second root of Fascism lies in the retarding of the world revolution by the treacherous attitude of the reformist leaders. Large numbers of the petty bourgeoisie, including even the middle classes, had discarded their war-time psychology for a certain sympathy with reformist socialism, hoping that the latter would bring about a reformation of society along democratic lines. They were disappointed in their hopes. They can now see that the reformist leaders are in benevolent accord with the bourgeoisie, and the worst of it is that these masses have now lost their faith not only in the reformist leaders, but in socialism as a whole.

These masses of disappointed socialist sympathisers are joined by large circles of the proletariat, of workers who have given up their faith not only in socialism, but also in their own class. Fascism has become a sort of refuge for the politically shelterless. In fairness it ought to be said that the Communists, too – except the Russians – bear part of the blame for the desertion of these elements to the Fascist ranks, because our actions at times failed to stir the masses profoundly enough. The obvious aim of the Fascists, when gaining support among the various elements of society, must have been, as a matter of course, to try and bridge over the class antagonism in the ranks of their own adherents, and the so-called authoritative State was to serve as a means to this end. Fascism now embraces such elements which may become very dangerous to the bourgeois order. Nevertheless, thus far these elements have been invariably overcome by the reactionary elements.

The bourgeoisie had seen the situation clearly from the start. The bourgeoisie wants to reconstruct capitalist economy. Under the present circumstances reconstruction of bourgeois class domination can be brought about only at the cost of increased exploitation of the proletariat by the bourgeoisie. The bourgeoisie is quite aware that the soft-speaking reformist socialists are fast losing their hold on the proletariat, and that there will be nothing for the bourgeoisie but to resort to violence against the proletariat. But the means of violence of the bourgeois States are beginning to fail. They therefore need a new organisation of violence, and this is offered to them by the hodge-podge conglomeration of Fascism. For this reason the bourgeoisie offers all the force at its command in the service of Fascism.

Fascism has diverse characteristics in different countries. Nevertheless it has two distinguishing features in all countries, namely, the pretence of a revolutionary programme, which is cleverly adapted to the interests and demands of the large masses, and, on the other hand, the application of the most brutal violence.

The classic instance is Italian Fascism. Industrial capital in Italy was not strong enough to reconstruct the ruined economy. It was not expected that the State would intervene to increase the power and the material possibilities of the industrial capital of Northern Italy. The State was giving all its attention to agrarian capital and to petty financial capital. The heavy industries, which had been artificially boosted during the war, collapsed when the war was over, and a wave of unprecedented unemployment set in. The pledges given to the soldiers could not be redeemed. All these circumstances created an extreme revolutionary situation. This revolutionary situation resulted, in the summer of 1920, in the occupation of the factories. Upon that occasion it was shown that the maturity of the revolution makes its first appearance among a small minority of the proletariat. The occupation of the factories was therefore bound to end in a tremendous defeat instead of becoming the starting point for revolutionary development. The reformist leaders of the trade unions acted the part of ignominious traitors, but at the same time it was shown that the proletariat possessed neither the will nor the power to march on towards revolution. Notwithstanding the reformist influence, there were forces at work among the proletariat which could become inconvenient to the bourgeoisie. The municipal elections, in which the social democrats gained a third of all the councils, were a signal of alarm to the bourgeoisie, who immediately started to seek for a force which could combat the revolutionary proletariat. It was just at that time that Mussolini had gained some importance with Fascismo.

After the defeat of the proletariat in the occupation of the factories, the number of the Fascisti was over 1,000 and great masses of the proletariat joined the Mussolini organisation. On the other hand, large masses of the proletariat had fallen into a state of indifference. The cause of the first success of the Fascisti was that it made its start with a revolutionary gesture. Its pretended aim was to fight to retain the revolutionary conquests of the revolutionary war, and for this reason they demanded a strong State which would be able to protect these revolutionary fruits of victory against the hostile interests of the various classes of society represented by the "old State." Its slogan was directed against all the exploiters, and hence also against the bourgeoisie. Fascism at that time was so radical that it even demanded the execution of Giolitti and the dethronement of the Italian dynasty. But Giolitti carefully refrained from using violence against Fascism, which seemed to him to be the lesser evil. To satisfy these Fascist clamours he dissolved Parliament. At that time Mussolini was still pretending to be a republican, and in an interview he declared that the

Fascist faction could not participate at the opening of the Italian parliament because of the monarchist ceremony accompanying it.

These utterances provoked a crisis in the Fascist Movement, which had been established as a party by a merger of the Mussolini adherents and the representatives of the monarchist organisation, and the executive of the new party was made up of an even number of members from both factions. The Fascist Party created a double-edged weapon for the corruption and terrorisation of the working class.

For the corruption of the working class the Fascist Trade Unions were created, the so-called corporations in which workers and employers were united. To terrorise the working class, the Fascist Party created the militant squads which had grown out of the punitive expeditions. Here it must be emphasised again that the tremendous treason of the Italian reformists during the general strike, which was the cause of the terrible defeat of the Italian proletariat, had given direct encouragement to the Fascists to capture the State. On the other hand, the mistakes of the Communist Party consisted in their regarding Fascism as merely a militarist and terrorist movement without any profound social basis.

Let us now examine what Fascism has done since the conquest of power for the fulfilment of its intended revolutionary programme, for the realisation of its promise to create a State without class. Fascism held out the promise of a new and better electoral law and of equal suffrage for women. The new suffrage law of Mussolini is in reality the worst restriction of the suffrage law to favour the Fascist Movement.

According to this law, two-thirds of all the seats must be given to the strongest party, and all the other parties together shall hold only one-third of the seats. Women's franchise has been nearly entirely eliminated. The right to vote is given only to a small group of propertied women and the so-called "war-distinguished" women. There is no longer any mention made of the promise of the economic parliament and National Assembly, nor of the abolition of the Senate which had been pledged so solemnly by the Fascists.

The same can be said about the pledges made in the social sphere. The Fascists had inscribed on their programme the eight-hour day, but the bill introduced by them provides so many exceptions that there is to be no eight-hour day in Italy. Nothing came also of the promised guarantee of wages. The destruction of the trade unions has enabled the employers to effect wage reductions of 20 to 30 per cent, and in some cases of even 50 to 60 per cent. Fascism had promised old age and invalid insurance. In practice the Fascist Government, for the sake of economy, has struck off the miserable 50,000,000 lire which had been set aside for this purpose in the budget. The workers were promised the right of technical participation in the administration of the factories. Today there is a law in Italy which proscribes the factory councils completely. The State enterprises are playing into the hands of private capital. The Fascist programme had contained a provision for a progressive income tax on capital, which was to some extent to act as a form of expropriation. In fact the opposite was done. Various taxes on luxuries were abolished, such as the automobile tax, for the pretended reason that it would restrict national production.

The indirect taxes were increased for the reason that this would curtail the home consumption and thus improve the possibilities for export. The Fascist Government also abrogated the law for the compulsory registration of transfers of securities, thus reintroducing the system of bearer-bonds and opening the door wide to the tax-evader. The schools were handed over to the clergy. Before capturing the State, Mussolini demanded a commission to inquire into war profits, of which 85 per cent were to be restored to the State.

When this commission had become uncomfortable for his financial backers, the heavy industrialists, he ordered that the commission should only submit a report to him, and whoever published any of the things that transpired in that commission would be punished with six months' imprisonment. Also in military matters Fascism failed to keep its promises. The army was promised to be restricted to territorial defence. In reality, the term of service for the standing army was increased from eight months to eighteen, which meant the increase of the armed forces from 250,000 to 350,000. The Royal Guards were abolished because they were too democratic to suit Mussolini. On the other hand, the carabinieri were increased from 65,000 to 90,000, and all the police troops were doubled. The Fascist organisations were transformed into a kind of national militia, which by latest accounts have now reached the number of 500,000. But the social differences have introduced an element of political contrast in the militia, which must lead to the eventual collapse of Fascism.

When we compare the Fascist programme with its fulfilment we can foresee already to-day the complete ideological collapse of Fascism in Italy. Political bankruptcy must inevitably follow in the wake of this ideological bankruptcy. Fascism is unable to keep together the forces which helped it to get into power. A clash of interests in many forms is already making itself felt. Fascism has not yet succeeded in making the old bureaucracy subservient to it. In the army there is also friction between the old officers and the new Fascist leaders. The differences between the various political parties are growing. Resistance against Fascism is increasing throughout the country. Class antagonism begins to permeate even the ranks of the

Fascists. The Fascists are unable to keep the promises which they made to the workers and to the Fascist Trade Unions. Wage reductions and dismissals of workers are the order of the day.

Thus it happens that the first protest against the Fascist trade union movement came from the ranks of the Fascists themselves. The workers will very soon come back to their class interest and class duty. We must not look upon Fascism as a united force capable of repelling our attack. It is rather a formation, which comprises many antagonistic elements, and will be disintegrated from within. But it would be dangerous to assume that the ideological and political disintegration of Fascism in Italy would be immediately followed by military disintegration. On the contrary, we must be prepared for Fascism to endeavour to keep alive by terrorist methods.

Therefore, the revolutionary Italian workers must be prepared for further serious struggles. It would be a great calamity if we were satisfied with the role of spectators of this process of disintegration. It is our duty to hasten this process with all the means at our disposal. This is not only the duty of the Italian proletariat, but also the duty of the German proletariat in the face of German Fascism.

After Italy, Fascism is strongest in Germany. As a consequence of the result of the war and of the failure of the revolution, the capitalist economy of Germany is weak, and in no other country is the contrast between the objective ripeness for revolution and the subjective unpreparedness of the working class as great as just now in Germany.

In no other country have the reformists so ignominiously failed as in Germany. Their failure is more criminal than the failure of any other party in the old International, because it is they who should have conducted the struggle for the emancipation of the proletariat with utterly different means in the country where the working-class organisations are older and better organised than anywhere else.

I am firmly convinced that neither the Peace Treaties nor the occupation of the Ruhr has given such a fillip to Fascism in Germany as the seizure of power by Mussolini. This has encouraged the German Fascists. The collapse of Fascism in Italy would greatly discourage the Fascists in Germany. We must not overlook one thing: the prerequisite for the overthrow of Fascism abroad is the overthrow of Fascism in every single country by the proletariat of these countries. It behoves us to overcome Fascism ideologically and politically. This imposes enormous tasks on us. We must realise that Fascism is a movement of the disappointed and of those whose existence is ruined. Therefore, we must endeavour either to win over or to neutralise those wide masses who are still in the Fascist camp. I wish to emphasise the importance of our realising that we must struggle ideologically for the possession

16

of the soul of these masses. We must realise that they are not only trying to escape from their present tribulations, but that they are longing for a new philosophy. We must come out of the narrow limits of our present activity. The Third International is, in contradistinction to the old International, an International of all races without any distinctions whatever. The Communist Parties must not only be the vanguard of the proletarian manual workers, but also the energetic defenders of the interests of the brain workers. They must be the leaders of all sections of society which are driven into opposition to bourgeois domination because of their interests and their expectations of the future. Therefore, I welcomed the proposal of Comrade Zinoviev (speaking at a session of the Enlarged Executive Committee of the Communist International in June of this year) to take up the struggle for the Workers' and Peasants' Government. I was jubilant when I read about it. This new slogan has a great significance for all countries.

We cannot dispense with it in the struggle for the overthrow of Fascism. It means that the salvation of the wide masses of the small peasantry will be achieved through Communism. We must not limit ourselves merely to carrying on a struggle for our political and economic programme. We must at the same time familiarise the masses with the ideals of Communism as a philosophy. If we do this, we shall show the way to a new philosophy to all those elements which have lost their bearings during the historical development of recent times. The necessary prerequisite for this is that, as we approach these masses, we also become organisationally, as a Party, a firmly welded unit. If we do not do that, we run the risk of falling into opportunism and of going bankrupt. We must adapt our methods of work to our new tasks. We must speak to the masses in a language which they can understand, without doing prejudice to our ideas. Thus, the struggle against Fascism brings forward a number of new tasks.

It behoves all the parties to carry out this task energetically and in conformity with the situation in their respective countries. However, we must bear in mind that it is not enough to overcome Fascism ideologically and politically.

The position of the proletariat as regards Fascism is at present one of self-defence. This self-defence of the proletariat must take the form of a struggle for its existence and its organisation.

The proletariat must have a well organised apparatus of self-defence. Whenever Fascism uses violence, it must be met with proletarian violence. I do not mean by this individual terrorist acts, but the violence of the organised revolutionary class struggle of the proletariat. Germany has made a beginning by organising factory "hundreds." This struggle can only be successful if there is a proletarian united front. The workers must unite for this struggle regardless of party. The self-defence of the proletariat is one of the greatest incentives for the establishment of the proletarian united front. Only by instilling class-consciousness into the soul of every worker will we succeed in preparing also for the military overthrow of Fascism, which, at this juncture, is absolutely necessary.

If we succeed in this, we may be sure that it will be soon all up with the capitalist system and with bourgeois power, regardless of any success of the general offensive of the bourgeoisie against the proletariat. The signs of disintegration, which are so palpably before our eyes, give us the conviction that the giant proletariat will again join in the revolutionary fray, and that its call to the bourgeois world will be: I am the strength, I am the will, in me you see the future!

Neither Fascism nor Liberalism: Sovietism!
Antonio Gramsci

In the political crisis of the liquidation of fascism the opposition bloc increasingly appears to be a factor of a secondary order. Its heterogeneous social composition, its hesitations, and its aversion for a struggle of the popular masses against the Fascist regime reduce its actions to a journalistic campaign and parliamentary intrigues, which impotently run up against the armed militia of the Fascist party.[3]

In the opposition movement to fascism the most important part has passed to the Liberal Party because the bloc has no other program to oppose to fascism than the old Liberal program of parliamentary bourgeois democracy, the return to the constitution, to legality, to democracy. In the discussion concerning the succession to fascism, according to the congress of the Liberal Party the Italian people is placed by the opposition before a choice: either fascism or liberalism; either a Mussolini government of bloody dictatorship or a Slandri, Gioliotti, Amendola, Turati, don Sturzo, or Vella government tending towards the reestablishment of the good old liberal Italian democracy, under whose mask the bourgeoisie will continue to exercise its exploitative rule.

The worker, the peasant, who for years has hated the fascism that oppresses him believes it necessary, in order to bring it down, to ally himself with the liberal bourgeoisie, to support those who in the past, when they were in power, supported and armed fascism against the workers and peasants, and who just a few months ago formed a sole bloc with fascism and shared in the responsibility for its crimes. And this is how the question of the liquidation of fascism is posed? No! The liquidation of fascism must be the liquidation of the bourgeoisie that created it.

When the Communist Party, in the days after the assassination of Matteoti, issued the slogan: "Down with the government of assassins! Dissolution of the Fascist militia!" it didn't think that the government of assassins should be replaced by a government of those who in all their policies had opened the way to and armed the assassins; it never

---

[3] Antonio Gramsci (January 22, 1891 – April 27, 1937) was an Italian philosopher, writer, politician and political theorist. A founding member and onetime leader of the Communist Party of Italy, he was imprisoned by Benito Mussolini's Fascist regime. This article appeared in L'Unità, October 7, 1924. Translated: by Mitchell Abidor

thought that Giolitti, Nitti, and Amendola, who were in power when the Fascist militia was formed, would be capable of disarming this militia which they had favored and armed against the working class.

In putting forth its slogan our party didn't intend to replace failing fascism with the old liberalism, whose opprobrious failure and definitive liquidation the March on Rome had signaled. The Communist Party, from the beginning of the crisis of fascism, affirmed that the working class and the peasants must be the gravediggers and the successors of those in power.

The action of the mass of industrial proletarians and peasants is necessary for the defeat of fascism, for the class struggle with all of its consequences. Without a doubt the proletariat should and must use, in its struggle against fascism, the contradictions and the struggles that have developed within the bourgeoisie and the petty-bourgeoisie. But without direct action fascism can never be brought down. Posing the problem in this way would mean, at the same time, clearly posing the question of the succession to fascism. With the defeat of fascism by the action of the worker and peasant masses liberalism will have no part in the succession: this right belongs to the government of the workers and peasants which alone will be capable of and will have the sincere determination to disarm the Fascist militia, arming the working class and the peasants.

At the current time it is a question of something other than the return of the constitution, to democracy and liberalism. These latter are mellifluous words that the bourgeoisie uses to mislead the workers of the city and the countryside in order to prevent the crisis from taking on its true character, that is the vengeance of the workers and peasants against the fascism that has suppressed them and against the liberalism that has misled them, and which just a few months ago collaborated or sought to collaborate (D'Aragona, Baldesi, etc) with Mussolini.

The Italian crisis can only be resolved through the action of the laboring masses. There is no possibility for the liquidation of fascism on the plain of parliamentary intrigues, only a compromise that leaves the bourgeoisie at the lead along with armed fascism at its service. Liberalism, even if inoculated with the glands of the reformist monkey, is powerless. It belongs to the past. And all the Don Struzos of Italy, united with the Turatis and the Vellas, will not succeed in returning to it the youth necessary for the liquidation of fascism.

A government of the classes of workers and peasants, which will not preoccupy itself either with the constitution or the sacred principles of liberalism, but which is determined to definitively defeat fascism, to disarm it and to defend the interests of the workers of the cities and the fields against all exploiters, this alone is the sole youthful force capable of liquidating a past of oppression, of exploitation and crime and of giving a future of true liberty to all who labour.

Today the Communist Party is the only one that repeats this truth to the proletariat. Its influence increases, its organization is developing, but the majority of the workers and peasants, dragged along by the Confederation of Labour and the Maximalist Party, in their turn advancing in the wake of the constitutional opposition, has not yet re-acquired its class consciousness, hasn't understood that the working and peasant class is the principal factor in the crisis because it has the irresistible numbers and the great force of youth. If it doesn't want to delude itself it must act on the plain of the class struggle as an independent force, which will soon be determinant, and not on the plain of class collaboration in order to do nothing but change the mask of the Italian bourgeoisie.

The essential task of our party consists is having penetrate among the workers and peasants this fundamental idea: only the class struggle of the mass of workers and peasants will defeat fascism. Only a government of workers and peasants can disarm the fascist militia. When these essential truths will have penetrated the spirit of the working and peasant masses by means of our tireless propaganda the workers of the factories and the fields, of whatever party, will understand the need to construct Worker and Peasant Committees for the defence of their class interests and for the struggle against fascism.

They will understand that these are the necessary instruments of the revolutionary struggle and of their will to replace the government of assassins with a government of workers and peasants. At the moment of the closing of the of the Liberal Congress, which seeks yet again to win over the working people, from one end to the other of Italy the workers and peasants answer their sonorous and empty chatter with: *Neither Fascism nor Liberalism: Sovietism!*

Fascism: What it is & How to Fight It
Leon Trotsky

Fascism -- What Is It?

What is fascism? The name originated in Italy. Were all the forms of counter-revolutionary dictatorship fascist or not (That is to say, prior to the advent of fascism in Italy)?[4]

The former dictatorship in Spain of Primo de Rivera, 1923-30, is called a fascist dictatorship by the Comintern. Is this correct or not? We believe that it is incorrect.

The fascist movement in Italy was a spontaneous movement of large masses, with new leaders from the rank and file. It is a plebian movement in origin, directed and financed by big capitalist powers. It issued forth from the petty bourgeoisie, the slum proletariat, and even to a certain extent from the proletarian masses; Mussolini, a former socialist, is a "self-made" man arising from this movement.

Primo de Rivera was an aristocrat. He occupied a high military and bureaucratic post and was chief governor of Catalonia. he accomplished his overthrow with the aid of state and military forces. The dictatorships of Spain and Italy are two totally different forms of dictatorship. It is necessary to distinguish between them. Mussolini had difficulty in reconciling many old military institutions with the fascist militia. This problem did not exist for Primo de Rivera.

The movement in Germany is analogous mostly to the Italian. It is a mass movement, with its leaders employing a great deal of socialist demagogy. This is necessary for the creation of the mass movement.

The genuine basis (for fascism) is the petty bourgeoisie. In Italy, it has a very large base -- the petty bourgeoisie of the towns and cities, and the peasantry. In Germany, likewise, there is a large base for fascism....

It may be said, and this is true to a certain extent, that the new middle class, the functionaries of the state, the private administrators,

---

[4] Leon Trotsky (7 November 1879 – 21 August 1940), was a Bolshevik revolutionary and Marxist theorist. He was one of the leaders of the Russian October Revolution, second only to Vladimir Lenin. During the early days of the Soviet Union, he served first as People's Commissar for Foreign Affairs and later as the founder and commander of the Red Army and People's Commissar of War. He was also among the first members of the Politburo. This article, "Fascism -- What Is It?" extracts from a letter to an English comrade, November 15 1931, printed in The Militant, January 16, 1932

etc., can constitute such a base. But this is a new question that must be analyzed....

In order to be capable of foreseeing anything with regard to fascism, it is necessary to have a definition of that idea. What is fascism? What are its base, its form, and its characteristics? How will its development take place? It is necessary to proceed in a scientific and Marxian manner.

How Mussolini Triumphed

At the moment that the "normal" police and military resources of the bourgeois dictatorship, together with their parliamentary screens, no longer suffice to hold society in a state of equilibrium -- the turn of the fascist regime arrives. Through the fascist agency, capitalism sets in motion the masses of the crazed petty bourgeoisie and the bands of declassed and demoralized lumpenproletariat -- all the countless human beings whom finance capital itself has brought to desperation and frenzy.[5]

From fascism the bourgeoisie demands a thorough job; once it has resorted to methods of civil war, it insists on having peace for a period of years. And the fascist agency, by utilizing the petty bourgeoisie as a battering ram, by overwhelming all obstacles in its path, does a thorough job. After fascism is victorious, finance capital directly and immediately gathers into its hands, as in a vice of steel, all the organs and institutions of sovereignty, the executive administrative, and educational powers of the state: the entire state apparatus together with the army, the municipalities, the universities, the schools, the press, the trade unions, and the co-operatives. When a state turns fascist, it does not mean only that the forms and methods of government are changed in accordance the patterns set by Mussolini -- the changes in this sphere ultimately play a minor role -- but it means first of all for the most part that the workers' organizations are annihilated; that the proletariat is reduced to an amorphous state; and that a system of administration is created which penetrates deeply into the masses and which serves to frustrate the independent crystallization of the proletariat. Therein precisely is the gist of fascism....

* * *

---

[5] From What Next? Vital Questions for the German Proletariat, 1932

Italian fascism was the immediate outgrowth of the betrayal by the reformists of the uprising of the Italian proletariat. From the time the [first world] war ended, there was an upward trend in the revolutionary movement in Italy, and in September 1920 it resulted in the seizure of factories and industries by the workers. The dictatorship of the proletariat was an actual fact; all that was lacking was to organize it and draw from it all the necessary conclusions. The social democracy took fright and sprang back. After its bold and heroic exertions, the proletariat was left facing the void. The disruption of the revolutionary movement became the most important factor in the growth of fascism. In September, the revolutionary advance came to a standstill; and November already witnessed the first major demonstration of the fascists (the seizure of Bologna[6]).

True, the proletariat, even after the September catastrophe, was capable of waging defensive battles. But the social democracy was concerned with only one thing: to withdraw the workers from combat at the cost of one concession after another. The social democracy hoped that the docile conduct of the workers would restore the "public opinion" of the bourgeoisie against the fascists. Moreover, the reformists even banked strongly upon the help of King Victor Emmanuel. To the last hour, they restrained the workers with might and main from giving battle to Mussolini's bands. It availed them nothing. The crown, along with the upper crust of the bourgeoisie, swung over to the side of fascism. Convinced at the last moment that fascism was not to be checked by obedience, the social democrats issued a call to the workers for a general strike. But their proclamation suffered a fiasco. The reformists had dampened the powder so long, in their fear lest it should explode, that when they finally with a trembling hand did apply a burning fuse to it, the powder did not catch.

Two years after its inception, fascism was in power. It entrenched itself thanks to the facts the first period of its overlordship coincided with a favorable economic conjuncture, which followed the depression

---

[6] The fascist campaign of violence began in Bologna, November 21, 1920. When the social-democratic councilmen, victorious in the municipal elections, emerged from city hall to present the new mayor, they were met by gunfire in which 10 were killed and 100 wounded. The fascists followed up with "punitive expeditions" into the surrounding countryside, a stronghold of the "Red Leagues". Blackshirt "action squadrons" in vehicles supplied by big landowners, took over villages in lightning raids, beating and killing leftist peasants and labor leaders, wrecking radical headquarters, and terrorizing the populace. Emboldened by their easy successes, the fascists then launched large-scale attacks in the big cities.

of 1921-22. The fascists crushed the retreating proletariat by the onrushing forces of the petty bourgeoisie. But this was not achieved at a single blow. Even after he assumed power, Mussolini proceeded on his course with due caution: he lacked as yet ready-made models. During the first two years, not even the constitution was altered. The fascist government took on the character of a coalition. In the meantime, the fascist bands were busy at work with clubs, knives, and pistols. Only thus was the fascist government created slowly, which meant the complete strangulation of all independent mass organizations.

Mussolini attained this at the cost of bureaucratizing the fascist party itself. After utilizing the onrushing forces of the petty bourgeoisie, fascism strangled it within the vice of the bourgeois state. Mussolini could not have done otherwise, for the disillusionment of the masses he had united was precipitating itself into the most immediate danger ahead. Fascism, become bureaucratic, approaches very closely to other forms of military and police dictatorship. It no longer possesses its former social support. The chief reserve of fascism -- the petty bourgeoisie -- has been depicted. Only historical inertia enables the fascist government to keep the proletariat in a state of dispersion and helplessness....

In its politics as regards Hitler, the German social democracy has not been able to add a single word: all it does is repeat more ponderously whatever the Italian reformists in their own time performed with greater flights of temperament. The latter explained fascism as a postwar psychosis; the German social democracy sees in it a "Versailles"[7] or crisis psychosis. In both instances, the reformists shut their eyes to the organic character of fascism as a mass movement growing out of the collapse of capitalism.

Fearful of the revolutionary mobilization of the workers, the Italian reformists banked all their hopes of the "state". Their slogan was, "Help! Victor Emmanuel, exert pressure!" The German social democracy lacks such a democratic bulwark as a monarch loyal to the constitution. So they must be content with a president -- "Help! Hindenburg[8], exert pressure!"

---

[7] The Versailles Treaty, imposed on Germany after WWI; its most hated feature was the unending tribute to the victorious allies in the form of "reparations" for war damages and losses. The "crisis" referred to in the above paragraph was the economic depression that swept the capitalist world after the Wall Street crash of 1929.

[8] Field Marshal Paul von Hindenburg (1847-1934), Junker general who gained fame in World War I and later became president of the Weimar Republic. In

While waging battle against Mussolini, that is, while retreating before him, Turati[9] let loose his dazzling motto, "One must have the manhood to be a coward." The German reformists are less frisky with their slogans. They demand "Courage under unpopularity" (*Mut zur Unpopularitaet*) -- which amounts to the same thing. One must not be afraid of the unpopularity which has been aroused by one's own cowardly temporizing with the enemy.

Identical causes produce identical effects. Were the march of events dependent upon the social-democratic party leadership, Hitler's career would be assured.

One must admit, however, that the German Communist Party has also learned little from the Italian experience.

The Italian Communist Party came into being almost simultaneously with fascism. But the same conditions of revolutionary ebb tide, which carried the fascists to power, served to deter the development of the Communist Party. It did not give itself an accounting as to the full sweep of the fascist danger; it lulled itself with revolutionary illusions; it was irreconcilably antagonistic to the policy of the united front; in short, it was stricken with all the infantile diseases. Small wonder! It was only two years old. In its eyes, fascism appeared to be only "capitalist reaction". The particular traits of fascism which spring from the mobilization of the petty bourgeoisie against the proletariat, the Communist Party was unable to discern. Italian comrades inform me that, with the sole exception of Gramsci[10], the Communist Party would not even allow for the possibility of the fascists' seizing power. Once the proletarian revolution had suffered defeat, once capitalism had held its ground and the counter-revolution had triumphed, how could there be any further kind of counter-revolutionary upheaval? How could the bourgeoisie rise up against itself! Such was the gist of the political orientation of the Italian

1932, the social democrats supported him for re-election as a "lesser evil" to the Nazis. He appointed Hitler chancellor in January 1933.

[9] Filippo Turati (1857-1937), leading reformist theoretician of the Italian Socialist Party.

[10] Antonio Gramsci (1891-1937): a founder of the Italian Communist Party, imprisoned by Mussolini in 1926, he died in prison 11 years later. He sent a letter from prison, in the name of the Italian party's political committee, protesting Stalin's campaign against the Left Opposition. Togliatti, then in Moscow as the Italian representative to the Comintern, suppressed the letter. Throughout the Stalin era, Gramsci's memory was deliberately effaced. In the period of de-Stalinization, however, he was "rediscovered" by the Italian Communist Party and officially enshrined as a hero and martyr. Since, there has been considerable international acclaim of his theoretical writings, particularly his prison notebooks.

Communist Party. Moreover, one must not lose sight of the fact that Italian fascism was then a new phenomenon, just in the process of formation; it would not have been an easy task even for a more experienced party to distinguish its specific traits.

The leadership of the German Communist Party today reproduces almost literally the position from which the Italian Communists took their point of departure; fascism is nothing else but capitalist reaction; from the point of view of the proletariat, the difference between divers types of capitalist reaction are meaningless. This vulgar radicalism is the less excusable because the German party is much older than the Italian was at a corresponding period; in addition, Marxism is enriched now by the tragic experience in Italy. To insist that fascism is already here, or to deny the very possibility of its coming to power, amounts politically to one and the same thing. By ignoring the specific nature of of fascism, the will to fight against it inevitably becomes paralyzed.

The brunt of the blame must be borne, of course, by the leadership of the Comintern. Italian Communists above all others were duty-bound to raise their voices in alarm. But Stalin, together with Manuilsky[11], compelled them to disavow the most important lessons of their own annihilation.

We have already observed with what diligent alacrity Ercoli[12] switched over to the position of social fascism -- i.e., to the position of passively waiting for the fascist victory in Germany.

The Fascist Danger Looms in Germany

The official press of the Comintern is now depicting the results of the [September 1930] German elections as a prodigious victory of Communism, which places on the order of the day the slogan of Soviet Germany.[13] The bureaucratic optimists do not want to reflect upon the meaning of the relation of forces which is disclosed by the election statistics. They examine the figure of the increased Communist vote

---

[11] Dmitri Manuilsky (1883-1952): Headed the Comintern from 1929 to 1934; his removal heralded switch from ultra-leftism to the opportunism of the Popular Front period. Later appeared on diplomatic stage, as delegate to United Nations.

[12] Ercoli. Comintern pen name of Palmiro Togliatti (1893-1964). Headed Italian Communist Party after Gramsci's imprisonment. He survived all zigzags in Comintern line, but after Stalin's death he criticized Stalin's rule as well some of its continuing features in the USSR and International Communist movement.

[13] From The Turn in the Communist International and the German Situation, 1930

independently of the revolutionary tasks created by the situation and the obstacles it sets up. The Communist Party received around 4,600,000 votes as against 3,300,000 in 1928. From the viewpoint of "normal" parliamentary mechanics, the gain of 1,300,000 votes is considerable, even if we take into consideration the rise in the total number of voters. But the gain of the party pales completely beside the leap of fascism from 800,000 to 6,400,000 votes. Of no less important significance for evaluation the elections is the fact that the social democracy, in spite of substantial losses, retained its basic cadres and still received a considerably greater number of workers' votes [8,600,000] than the Communist Party.

Meanwhile, if we should ask ourselves, "What combination of international and domestic circumstances could be capable of turning the working class towards Communism with greater velocity?" we could not find an example of more favorable circumstances for such a turn than the situation in present-day Germany: Young's noose[14], the economic crisis, the disintegration of the rules, the crisis of parliamentarism, the terrific self-exposure of the social democracy in power. From the viewpoint of these concrete historical circumstances, the specific gravity of the German Communist Party in the social life of the country, in spite of the gain of 1,300,000 votes, remains proportionately small.

The weakness of the position of Communism, inextricably bound up with the policy and regime of the Comintern, is revealed more clearly if we compare the present social weight of the Communist Party with those concrete and unpostponable tasks which the present historical circumstances put before it.

It is true that the Communist Party itself did not expect such a gain. But this proves that under the blows of mistakes and defeats, the leadership of the Communist parties has become unused to big aims and perspectives. If yesterday it underestimated its own possibilities, then today it once more underestimates the difficulties. In this way, one danger is multiplied by another.

In the meantime, the first characteristic of a really revolutionary party is -- to be able to look reality in the face.

* * *

---

[14] "Young's noose": a reference to the Young Plan. After Owen D. Young, American big businessman, who was Agent-General for the German Reparations during the 1920s. In summer of 1929, he was chairman of the conference which adopted his plan, which replaced the unsuccessful Dawes Plan, to "facilitate" Germany's payment of reparations as per the Treaty of Versailles.

In order that the social crisis may bring about the proletarian revolution, it is necessary that, besides other conditions, a decisive shift of the petty bourgeois classes occurs in the direction of the proletariat. This gives the proletariat a chance to put itself at the head of the nation as its leader.

The last election revealed -- and this is where its principle symptomatic significance lies -- a shift in the opposite direction. Under the blow of the crisis, the petty bourgeoisie swung, not in the direction of the proletarian revolution, but in the direction of the most extreme imperialist reaction, pulling behind it considerable sections of the proletariat.

The gigantic growth of National Socialism is an expression of two factors: a deep social crisis, throwing the petty bourgeois masses off balance, and the lack of a revolutionary party that would be regarded by the masses of the people as an acknowledged revolutionary leader. If the communist Party is the party of revolutionary hope, then fascism, as a mass movement, is the party of counter-revolutionary despair. When revolutionary hope embraces the whole proletarian mass, it inevitably pulls behind it on the road of revolution considerable and growing sections of the petty bourgeoisie. Precisely in this sphere the election revealed the opposite picture: counter-revolutionary despair embraced the petty bourgeois mass with such a force that it drew behind it many sections of the proletariat....

Fascism in Germany has become a real danger, as an acute expression of the helpless position of the bourgeois regime, the conservative role of the social democracy in this regime, and the accumulated powerlessness of the Communist Party to abolish it. Whoever denies this is either blind or a braggart....

The danger acquires particular acuteness in connection with the question of the tempo of development, which does not depend upon us alone. The malarial character of the political curve revealed by the election speaks for the fact that the tempo of development of the national crisis may turn out to be very speedy. In other words, the course of events in the very near future may resurrect in Germany, on a new historical plane, the old tragic contradiction between the maturity of a revolutionary situation, on the one hand, and the weakness and strategical impotence of the revolutionary party, on the other. This must be said clearly, openly and, above all, in time.

* * *

Can the strength of the conservative resistance of the social-democratic workers be calculated beforehand? It cannot. In the light of the events of the past year, this strength seems to be gigantic. But the truth is that what helped most of all to weld together social democracy was the wrong policy of the Communist Party, which found its highest generalization in the absurd theory of social fascism. To measure the real resistance of the social democratic ranks, a different measuring instrument is required, that is, a correct Communist tactic. With this condition -- and it is not a small condition -- the degree of internal unity of the social democracy can be revealed in a comparatively brief period.

In a different form, what has been said above also applies to fascism: It emanated, aside from the other conditions present, in the tremblings of the Zinoviev-Stalin strategy.[15] What is its force for offensive? What is its stability? has it reached its culminating point, as the optimists ex-officio[16] assure us, or is it only on the first step of the ladder? This cannot be foretold mechanically. It can be determined only through action. Precisely in regard to fascism, which is a razor in the hands of the class enemy, the wrong policy of the Comintern may produce fatal results in a brief period. On the other hand, a correct policy -- not in such a short period, it is true -- can undermine the positions of fascism....

If the Communist Party, in spite of the exceptionally favorable circumstances, has proved powerless seriously to shake the structure of the social democracy with the aid of the formula of "social fascism", then real fascism now threatens this structure, no longer with wordy formulae of so-called radicalism, but with the chemical formulas of explosives. No matter how true it is that the social democracy by its whole policy prepared the blossoming of fascism, it is no less true that fascism comes forward as a deadly threat primarily to that same social democracy, all of whose magnificence is inextricably bound with parliamentary-democratic-pacifist forms and methods of government...

The policy of a united front of the workers against fascism flows from this situation. It opens up tremendous possibilities to the

---

[15] Gregory Y. Zinoviev (1883-1936), chairman of the Comintern from its founding in 1919 till his removal by Stalin in 1926. After Lenin's death, Zinoviev and Kamenev made a bloc with Stalin (the Troika) against Trotsky and dominated the Soviet party. In the period of the Zinoviev-Stalin domination of the Comintern, an opportunist line led to a series of defeats and missed opportunities, most notably the calling off of the German revolution of 1923. After breaking with Stalin, Zinoviev united his following with the Trotskyist Left Opposition. But in 1928, after the expulsion from the party of the United Opposition, Zinoviev capitulated to Stalin. Readmitted to the party, he was expelled again in 1932. After disavowal of all critical views, he was again readmitted, but in 1934, he was expelled and imprisoned. He "confessed" at the first of the great Moscow Trials in 1936 and was executed.
[16] Comintern and Communist Party officials.

Communist Party. A condition for success, however, is the rejection of the theory and practice of "social fascism", the harm of which becomes a positive measure under the present circumstances.

The social crisis will inevitably produce deep cleavages within the social democracy. The radicalization of the masses will affect the social democrats. We will inevitably have to make agreements with various social-democratic organizations and factions against fascism, putting definite conditions in this connection to the leaders, before the eyes of the masses.... We must return from the empty official phrase about the united front to the policy of the united front as it was formulated by Lenin and always applied by the Bolsheviks in 1917.

An Aesop Fable

A cattle dealer once drove some bulls to the slaughterhouse. And the butcher came night with his sharp knife.[17]

"Let us close ranks and jack up this executioner on our horns," suggested one of the bulls.

"If you please, in what way is the butcher any worse than the dealer who drove us hither with his cudgel?" replied the bulls, who had received their political education in Manuilsky's institute. [The Comintern.]

"But we shall be able to attend to the dealer as well afterwards!"

"Nothing doing," replied the bulls firm in their principles, to the counselor. "You are trying, from the left, to shield our enemies -- you are a social-butcher yourself."

And they refused to close ranks.

The German Cops And Army

In case of actual danger, the social democracy banks not on the "Iron Front"[18] but on the Prussian police. It is reckoning without its host! The fact that the police was originally recruited in large numbers from among social-democratic workers is absolutely meaningless.

---

[17] This and the following item are from What Next? Vital Question for the German Proletariat, 1932.

[18] A bloc between several big trade unions and bourgeois "republican" groups with little or no following or prestige among the masses. It was created by the social democrats toward the end of 1931. Combat groups called the Iron Fist were set up within the unions, and workers' sports organizations were brought into the Iron Front. However, its first parades and rallies, at which thousands of workers raised their fists, shouted "Freedom", and swore to defend democracy. The masses in the Social Democratic Party and unions really believed that this organization would be used to stop Hitler. It was not.

Consciousness is determined by environment even in this instance. The worker who becomes a policeman in the service of the capitalist state, is a bourgeois cop, not a worker. Of late years, these policemen have had to do much more fighting with revolutionary workers than with Nazi students. Such training does not fail to leave its effects. And above all: every policeman knows that though governments may change, the police remains.

In its New Year's issue, the theoretical organ of the social democracy, *Der Freie Wort* (what a wretched sheet!), prints an article in which the policy of "toleration" is expounded in its highest sense. Hitler, it appears, can never come to power against the police and the Reichswehr [German army]. Now, according to the constitution, the Reichswehr is under the command of the president of the Republic. Therefore fascism, it follows, is not dangerous so long as a president faithful to the constitution remains at the head of the government. Bruening's regime[19] must be supported until the presidential elections so that a constitutional president may then be elected, through an alliance with the parliamentary bourgeoisie; and thereby Hitler's road to power will be blocked for another seven years....

The politicians of reformism, these dexterous wire-pullers, artful intriguers and careerists, expert parliamentary and ministerial machinators, are no sooner thrown out of their habitual sphere by the course of events, no sooner are the placed face to face with momentous contingencies than they reveal themselves to be -- there is no milder expression for it -- inept bodies.

To rely upon a president is only to rely upon "the government"! Faced with the impending clash between the proletariat and the fascist petty bourgeoisie -- two camps which together comprise the crushing majority of the German nation -- these Marxists from the *Vorwaerts* [principal social-democratic newspaper] yelp for the nightwatchman to come to their aid, "Help! Government, exert pressure!" (*Staat, greif zu!)*

---

[19] Heinrich Bruening was chancellor from 1930-32. Regular parliamentary government in Germany ended in March 1930. There followed a series of Bonapartist regimes -- Bruening, von Papen, von Schleicher, i.e., chancellors ruling not by ordinary parliamentary procedures but by "emergency" decrees. These Bonapartist figures presented themselves as political saviors needed to get the country through its crisis, and thus as above class and party. They depended not on the old bourgeois democratic party system but on their command of the police, army, and government bureaucracy. Pretending to be saving the nation from the dangers on both the left (socialists and communists) and the right (fascists), they struck their heaviest blows against the left, since their primary interest was saving capitalism.

Bourgeoisie, Petty Bourgeoisie, and Proletariat

Any serious analysis of the political situation must take as its point of departure the mutual relations among the three classes: the bourgeoisie, the petty bourgeoisie (including the peasantry), and the proletariat.[20]

The economically powerful big bourgeoisie, in itself, represents an infinitesimal minority of the nation. To enforce its domination, it must ensure a definite mutual relationship with the petty bourgeoisie and, through its mediation, with the proletariat.

To understand the dialectic of the relation among the three classes, we must differentiate three historical stages: at the dawn of capitalistic development, when the bourgeoisie required revolutionary methods to solve its tasks; in the period of bloom and maturity of the capitalist regime, when the bourgeoisie endowed its domination with orderly, pacific, conservative, democratic forms; finally, at the decline of capitalism, when the bourgeoisie is forced to resort to methods of civil war against proletariat to protect its right of exploitation.

The political programs characteristic of these three stages -- JACOBINISM [left wing of petty bourgeois forces in Great French Revolution; in most revolutionary phase, led by Robespierre], reformist DEMOCRACY (social democracy included), and FASCISM -- are basically programs of petty bourgeois currents. This fact alone, more than anything else, shows of what tremendous -- rather, of what decisive -- importance the self-determination of the petty bourgeois masses of the people is for the whole fate of bourgeois society.

Nevertheless, the relationship between the bourgeoisie and its basic social support, the petty bourgeoisie, does not at all rest upon reciprocal confidence and pacific collaboration. In its mass, the petty bourgeoisie is an exploited and disenfranchised class. It regards the bourgeoisie with envy and often with hatred. The bourgeoisie, on the other hand, while utilizing the support of the petty bourgeoisie, distrusts the latter, for it very correctly fears its tendency to break down the barriers set up for it from above.

While they were laying out and clearing the road for bourgeois development, the Jacobins engaged, at every step, in sharp clashes with the bourgeoisie. They served it in intransigent struggle against it. After they had culminated their limited historical role, the Jacobins fell, for the domination of capital was predetermined.

For a whole series of stages, the bourgeoisie entrenched its power under the form of parliamentary democracy. Even then, not peacefully

---

[20] From The Only Road for Germany written September 1932, published in the USA April 1933

and not voluntarily. The bourgeoisie was mortally afraid of universal suffrage. But in the last instance, it succeeded, with the aid of a combination of violent measures and concessions, of privations and reforms, in subordinating within the framework of formal democracy not only the petty bourgeoisie but in considerable measure also the proletariat, by means of the new petty bourgeoisie -- the labour aristocracy. In August 1914, the imperialist bourgeoisie was able, with the means of parliamentary democracy, to lead millions of workers and peasants into the war.[21]

But precisely with the war begins the distinct decline of capitalism and, above all, of its democratic form of domination. It is now no longer a matter of new reforms and alms, but of cutting down and abolishing the old ones. Therewith the bourgeoisie comes into conflict into only with the institutions of proletarian democracy (trade unions and political parties) but also with parliamentary democracy, within the framework of which arose the labour organizations. Therefore, the campaign against "Marxism" on the one hand and against democratic parliamentarism on the other.

But just as the summits of the liberal bourgeoisie in its time were unable, by their own force alone, to get rid of feudalism, monarchy, and the church, so the magnates of finance capital are unable, by their force alone, to cope with the proletariat. They need the support of the petty bourgeoisie. For this purpose, it must be whipped up, put on its feet, mobilized, armed. But this method has its dangers. While it makes use of fascism, the bourgeoisie nevertheless fears it. Pilsudski was forced, in May 1926, to save bourgeois society by a coup d'etat directed against the traditional parties of the Polish bourgeoisie. The matter went so far that the official leader of the Polish Communist Party, Warski, who came over from Rosa Luxemburg not to Lenin but to Stalin, took the coup d'etat of Pilsudski to be the road of the "revolutionary democratic dictatorship" and called upon the workers to support Pilsudski.[22]

---

[21] August 4, 1914: collapse of the Second International. The German Social-Democratic Party representatives in the Reichstag voted for the war budget of the imperialist governments; on the same day, representatives of the French Socialist Party did likewise in the Chamber of Deputies.

[22] Joseph Pilsudski (1876-1935): Originally a socialist with nationalistic views, in 1920 he led the anti-Soviet forces in Poland; in 1926, he led a coup d'etat and established a fascist dictatorship. Warski: Friend of Rosa Luxemburg, he supported her differences with the Bolsheviks. When Comintern zigzagged to the left in its "Third Period" phase, Warski was demoted from leadership in the Polish Communist Party, but not expelled. He disappeared in the USSR during the great purge of 1936-38. Rosa Luxemburg (1870-1919): Great

At the session of the Polish Commission of the Executive Committee of the Communist International on July 2, 1926, the author of these lines said on the subject of the events in Poland:

"Taken as a whole, the Pilsudski overthrow is the petty bourgeois, 'plebian' manner of solving the burning problems of bourgeois society in its state of decomposition and decline. We have here already a direct resemblance to Italian fascism.

"These two currents indubitably possess common features: they recruit their shock troops first of all from the petty bourgeoisie; Pilsudski as well as Mussolini worked with extra-parliamentary means, with open violence, with the methods of civil war; both were concerned not with the destruction but with the preservation of bourgeois society. While they raised the petty bourgeoisie on its feet, they openly aligned themselves, after the seizure of power, with the big bourgeoisie. Involuntarily, a historical generalization comes up here, recalling the evaluation given by Marx of Jacobinism as the plebian method of settling accounts with the feudal enemies of the bourgeoisie.... That was in the period of the rise of the bourgeoisie. Now we must say, in the period of the decline of bourgeois society, the bourgeoisie again needs the 'plebian' method of resolving its no longer progressive but entirely reactionary tasks. In this sense, fascism is a caricature of Jacobinism.

"The bourgeoisie is incapable of maintaining itself in power by the means and methods of the parliamentary state created by itself; it needs fascism as a weapon of self-defence, at least in critical instances. Nevertheless, the bourgeoisie does not like the 'plebian' method of resolving its tasks. It was always hostile of Jacobinism, which cleared the road for the development of bourgeois society with its blood. The fascists are immeasurably closer to the decadent bourgeoisie than the Jacobins were to the rising bourgeoisie. Nevertheless, the sober bourgeoisie does not look very favorably even upon the fascist mode of resolving its tasks, for the concussions, although they are brought forth in the interests of bourgeois society, are linked up with dangers to it. Therefore, the opposition between fascism and the bourgeois parties.

"The big bourgeoisie likes fascism as little as a man with aching molars likes to have his teeth pulled. The sober circles of bourgeois society have followed with misgivings the work of the dentist

---

revolutionary theoretician and leader. Originally active in socialist movement of her native Poland, she later became a leader of the left wing of the German Social-Democratic Party. She and Karl Liebknecht were imprisoned for opposing World War I. After their release, they led the Spartakusbund. Both were arrested and assassinated during the unsuccessful revolution of 1919.

Pilsudski, but in the last analysis they have become reconciled to the inevitable, though with threats, with horse-trades and all sorts of bargaining. Thus the petty bourgeoisie's idol of yesterday becomes transformed into the gendarme of capital."

To this attempt at marking out the historical place of fascism as the political reliever of the social democracy, there was counterposed the theory of social fascism. At first it could appear as a pretentious, blustering, but harmless stupidity. Subsequent events have shown what a pernicious influence the Stalinist theory actually exercised on the entire development of the Communist International.

Does it follow from the historical role of Jacobinism, of democracy, and of fascism, that the petty bourgeoisie is condemned to remain a tool in the hands of capital to the end of its days? It things were so, then the dictatorship of the proletariat would be impossible in a number of countries in which the petty bourgeoisie constitutes the majority of the nation and, more than that, it would be rendered extremely difficult in other countries in which the petty bourgeoisie represents an important minority. Fortunately, things are not so. The experience of the Paris Commune [first "dictatorship of the proletariat", March 18, 1871] first showed, at least within the limits of one city, just as the experience of the October Revolution [Russian Revolution of 1917] has shown after it on a much larger scale and over an incomparably longer period, that the alliance of the petty bourgeoisie and the big bourgeoisie is not indissoluble. Since the petty bourgeoisie is incapable of an independent policy (that is also why the petty bourgeois "democratic dictatorship" is unrealizable), no other choice is left for it than that between the bourgeoisie and the proletariat.

In the epoch of the rise, the growth, and the bloom of capitalism, the petty bourgeoisie, despite acute outbreaks of discontent, generally marched obediently in the capitalist harness. Nor could it do anything else. But under the conditions of capitalist disintegration, and of the impasse in the economic situation, the petty bourgeoisie strives, seeks, attempts to tear itself loose from the fetters of the old masters and rulers of society. It is quite capable of linking up its fates with that of the proletariat. For that, only one thing is needed: the petty bourgeoisie must acquired faith in the ability of the proletariat to lead society onto a new road. The proletariat can inspire this faith only by its strength, by the firmness of its actions, by a skillful offensive against the enemy, by the success of its revolutionary policy.

But, woe, if the revolutionary party does not measure up to the height of the situation! The daily struggle of the proletariat sharpens the instability of bourgeois society. The strikes and the political disturbances aggravated the economic situation of the country. The petty bourgeoisie could reconcile itself temporarily to the growing privations, if it arrived by experience at the conviction that the proletariat is in a position to lead it onto a new road. But if the revolutionary party, in spite of a class struggle becoming incessantly more accentuated, proves time and again to be incapable of uniting the working class about it, if it vacillates, becomes confused, contradicts itself, then the petty bourgeoisie loses patience and begins to look upon the revolutionary workers as those responsible for its own misery. All the bourgeois parties, including the social democracy, turn its thoughts in this very direction. When the social crisis takes on an intolerable acuteness, a particular party appears on the scene with the direct aim of agitating the petty bourgeoisie to a white heat and of directing its hatred and its despair against the proletariat. In Germany, this historical function is fulfilled by national Socialism (Nazism), a broad current whose ideology is composed of all the putrid vapors of disintegrating bourgeois society.

The Collapse of Bourgeois Democracy

After the war, a series of brilliantly victorious revolutions occurred in Russia, Germany, Austria-Hungary, and later in Spain. But it was only in Russia that the proletariat took full power into its hands, expropriated its exploiters, and knew how to create and maintain a workers' state. Everywhere else the proletariat, despite its victory, stopped halfway because of the mistakes of its leadership. As a result, power slipped from its hands, shifted from left to right, and fell prey to fascism. In a series of other countries, power passed into the hands of a military dictatorship. Nowhere were the parliaments capable of reconciling class contradictions and assuring the peaceful development of events. Conflicts were solved arms in hand.[23]

The French people for a long time thought that fascism had nothing whatever to do with them. They had a republic in which all questions were dealt with by the sovereign people through the exercise of universal suffrage. But on February 6, 1934, several thousand fascists and royalists, armed with revolvers, clubs, and razors, imposed upon the country the reactionary government of Doumergue[24], under whose protection the fascist bands continue to grow and arm themselves. What does tomorrow hold?

---

[23] This and the following two articles are from Whither France?, 1934
[24] Gaston Doumergue: Bonapartist premier of France. Succeeded Edouard Daladier. Daladier government fell the day after the fascist riots of February 6, 1934.

Of course, in France, as in certain other European countries (England, Belgium, Holland, Switzerland, the Scandinavian countries), there still exist parliaments, elections, democratic liberties, or their remnants. But in all these countries, the same historic laws operate, the laws of capitalist decline. If the means of production remain in the hands of a small number of capitalists, there is no way out for society. It is condemned to go from crisis to crisis, from need to misery, from bad to worse. In the various countries, the decrepitude and disintegration of capitalism are expressed in diverse forms and at unequal rhythms. But the basic features of the process are the same everywhere. The bourgeoisie is leading its society to complete bankruptcy. It is capable of assuring the people neither bread nor peace. This is precisely why it cannot any longer tolerate the democratic order. It is forced to smash the workers and peasants by the use of physical violence. The discontent of the workers and peasants, however, cannot be brought to an end by the police alone. Moreover, if it often impossible to make the army march against the people. It begins by disintegrating and ends with the passage of a large section of the soldiers over to the people's side. That is why finance capital is obliged to create special armed bands, trained to fight the workers just as certain breeds of dog are trained to hunt game. The historic function of fascism is to smash the working class, destroy its organizations, and stifle political liberties when the capitalists find themselves unable to govern and dominate with the help of democratic machinery.

The fascists find their human material mainly in the petty bourgeoisie. The latter has been entirely ruined by big capital. There is no way out for it in the present social order, but it knows of no other. Its dissatisfaction, indignation, and despair are diverted by the fascists away from big capital and against the workers. It may be said that fascism is the act of placing the petty bourgeoisie at the disposal of its most bitter enemies. In this way, big capital ruins the middle classes and then, with the help of hired fascist demagogues, incites the despairing petty bourgeoisie against the worker. The bourgeois regime can be preserved only by such murderous means as these. For how long? Until it is overthrown by proletarian revolution.

Does The Petty Bourgeoisie Fear Revolution?

Parliamentary cretins, who consider themselves connoisseurs of the people, like to repeat:

"One must not frighten the middle classes with revolution. They do not like extremes."

38

In this general form, this affirmation is absolutely false. Naturally, the petty proprietor prefers order so long as business is going well and so long as he hopes that tomorrow it will go better.

But when this hope is lost, he is easily enraged and is ready to give himself over to the most extreme measures. Otherwise, how could he have overthrown the democratic state and brought fascism to power in Italy and Germany? The despairing petty bourgeois sees in fascism, above all, a fighting force against big capital, and believes that, unlike the working-class parties which deal only in words, fascism will use force to establish more "justice". The peasant and the artisan are in their manner realists. They understand that one cannot forego the use of force.

It is false, thrice false, to affirm that the present petty bourgeoisie is not going to the working-class parties because it fears "extreme measures". Quite the contrary. The lower petty bourgeoisie, its great masses, only see in the working-class parties parliamentary machines. They do not believe in their strength, nor in their capacity to struggle, nor in their readiness this time to conduct the struggle to the end.

And if this is so, is it worth the trouble to replace the democratic capitalist representatives by their parliamentary confreres on the left? That is how the semi-exploited, ruined, and discontented proprietor reasons of feels. Without an understanding of this psychology of the peasants, the artisans, the employees, the petty functionaries, etc. -- a psychology which flows from the social crisis -- it is impossible to elaborate a correct policy. The petty bourgeoisie is economically dependent and politically atomized. That is why it cannot conduct an independent policy. It needs a "leader" who inspires it with confidence. This individual or collective leadership, i.e., a personage or party, can be given to it by one or the other of the fundamental classes -- either the big bourgeoisie or the proletariat. Fascism unties and arms the scattered masses. Out of human dust, it organizes combat detachments. It thus gives the petty bourgeoisie the illusion of being an independent force. It begins to imagine that it will really command the state. It is not surprising that these illusions and hopes turn the head of the petty bourgeoisie!

But the petty bourgeoisie can also find a leader in the proletariat. This was demonstrated in Russia and partially in Spain. In Italy, in Germany, and in Austria, the petty bourgeoisie gravitated in this direction. But the parties of the proletariat did not rise to their historic task.

To bring the petty bourgeoisie to its side, the proletariat must win its confidence. And for that it must have confidence in its own strength.

It must have a clear program of action and must be ready to struggle for power by all possible means. Tempered by it revolutionary party for a decisive and pitiless struggle, the proletariat says to the peasants and petty bourgeoisie of the cities:

"We are struggling for power. Here is our program. We are ready to discuss with you changes in this program. We will employ violence only against big capital and its lackeys, but with you toilers, we desire to conclude an alliance on the basis of a given program."

The peasants will understand such language. Only, they must have faith in the capacity of the proletariat to seize power.

But for that it is necessary to purge the united front of all equivocation, of all indecision, of all hollow phrases. It is necessary to understand the situation and to place oneself seriously on the revolutionary road.

The Workers' Militia and its Opponents

To struggle, it is necessary to conserve and strengthen the instrument and the means of struggle -- organizations, the press, meetings, etc. Fascism [in France] threatens all of that directly and immediately. It is still too weak for the direct struggle for power, but it is strong enough to attempt to beat down the working-class organizations bit by bit, to temper its bands in its attacks, and to spread dismay and lack of confidence in their forces in the ranks of the workers.

Fascism finds unconscious helpers in all those who say that the "physical struggle" is impermissible or hopeless, and demand of Doumergue the disarmament of his fascist guard. Nothing is so dangerous for the proletariat, especially in the present situation, as the sugared poison of false hopes. Nothing increases the insolence of the fascists so much as "flabby pacificism" on the part of the workers' organizations. Nothing so destroys the confidence of the middle classes in the working-class as temporizing, passivity, and the absence of the will to struggle.

Le Populaire [the Socialist Party paper] and especially [the Communist Party newspaper] write every day:

"The united front is a barrier against fascism";

"the united front will not permit...";

"the fascists will not dare", etc.

These are phrases. It is necessary to say squarely to the workers, Socialists, and Communists: do not allow yourselves to be lulled by the phrases of superficial and irresponsible journalists and orators. It is a question of our heads and the future of socialism. It is not that we deny the importance of the united front. We demanded it when the leaders of both parties were against it. The united front opens up numerous possibilities, but nothing more. In itself, the united front decides nothing. Only the struggle of the masses decides. The untied front will reveal its value when Communist detachments will come to the help of Socialist detachments and vice versa in the case of an attack by the fascist bands against *Le Populaire* or *l'Humanite*. But for that, proletarian combat detachments must exist and be educated, trained, and armed. And if there is not an organization of defence, i.e., a workers' militia, *Le Populaire* or *l'Humanite* will be able to write as many articles as they like on the omnipotence of the united front, but the two papers will find themselves defenceless before the first well-prepared attack of the fascists.

We propose to make a critical study of the "arguments" and the "theories" of the opponents of the workers' militia who are very numerous and influential in the two working-class parties.

"We need mass self-defence and not the militia," we are often told.

But what is this "mass self-defence" without combat organizations, without specialized cadres, without arms? To give over the defence against fascism to unorganized and unprepared masses left to themselves would be to play a role incomparably lower than the role of Pontius Pilate. To deny the role of the militia is to deny the role of the vanguard. Then why a party? Without the support of the masses, the militia is nothing. But without organized combat detachments, the most heroic masses will be smashed bit by bit by the fascist gangs. It is nonsense to counterpose the militia to self-defence. The militia is an organ of self-defence.

"To call for the organization of a militia," say some opponents who, to be sure, are the least serious and honest, "is to engage in provocation."

This is not an argument but an insult. If the necessity for the defence of the workers' organizations flows from the whole situation, how then can one not call for the creation of the militia? Perhaps they mean to say that the creation of a militia "provokes" fascist attacks and government repression. In that case, this is an absolutely reactionary argument. Liberalism has always said to the workers that by their class struggle they "provoke" the reaction.

The reformists repeated this accusation against the Marxists, the Mensheviks against the Bolsheviks. These accusations reduced themselves, in the final analysis, to the profound thought that if the oppressed do not balk, the oppressors will not be obliged to beat them. This is the philosophy of Tolstoy and Gandhi but never that of Marx and Lenin. If *l'Humanite* wants hereafter to develop the doctrine of "non-resistance to evil by violence", it should take for its symbol not the hammer and sickle, emblem of the October Revolution, but the pious goat, which provides Gandhi with his milk.

"But the arming of the workers is only opportune in a revolutionary situation, which does not yet exist."

This profound argument means that the workers must permit themselves to be slaughtered until the situation becomes revolutionary. Those who yesterday preached the "third period"[25] do not want to see what is going on before their eyes. The question of arms itself has come forward only because the "peaceful", "normal", "democratic" situation has given way to a stormy, critical, and unstable situation which can transform itself into a revolutionary, as well as a counter-revolutionary, situation.

This alternative depends above all on whether the advanced workers will allow themselves to be attacked with impunity and defeated bit by bit or will reply to every blow by two of their own, arousing the courage of the oppressed and uniting them around their banner. A revolutionary situation does not fall from the skies. It takes form with the active participation of the revolutionary class and its party.

The French Stalinists now argue that the militia did not safeguard the German proletariat from defeat. Only yesterday they completely denied any defeat in Germany and asserted that the policy of the German Stalinists was correct from beginning to end. Today, they see the entire evil in the German workers' militia (Rote Front) [i.e., Red Front Fighters: Communist-dominated militia banned by the social-democratic government after the Berlin May Day riots of 1929]. Thus, from one error they fall into a diametrically opposite one, no less monstrous. The militia, in itself, does not settle the question. A correct policy is necessary. Meanwhile, the policy of Stalinism in Germany ("social fascism is the chief enemy"), the split in the trade unions, the flirtation with nationalism, putschism) fatally led to the isolation of the proletarian vanguard and to its shipwreck. With an utterly worthless strategy, no militia could have saved the situation.

It is nonsense to say that, in itself, the organization of the militia leads to adventures, provokes the enemy, replaces the political struggle by physical struggle, etc. In all these phrases, there is nothing but political cowardice.

---

[25] "The Third Period": According to the Stalinist schema, this was the "final period of capitalism", the period of its immediately impending demise and replacement by soviets. The period is notable for the Communists' ultra-left and adventurist tactics, notably the concept of social-fascism.

The militia, as the strong organization of the vanguard, is in fact the surest defence against adventures, against individual terrorism, against bloody spontaneous explosions.

The militia is at the same time the only serious way of reducing to a minimum the civil war that fascism imposes upon the proletariat. Let the workers, despite the absence of a "revolutionary situation", occasionally correct the "papa's son" patriots in their own way, and the recruitment of new fascist bands will become incomparably more difficult.

But here the strategists, tangled in their own reasoning, bring forward against us still more stupefying arguments. We quote textually:

"If we reply to the revolver shots of the fascists with other revolver shots," writes *l'Humanite* of October 23 [1934], "we lose sight of the fact that fascism is the product of the capitalist regime and that in fighting against fascism it is the entire system which we face."

It is difficult to accumulate in a few lines greater confusion or more errors. It is impossible to defend oneself against the fascists because they are -- "a product of the capitalist regime". That means, we have to renounce the whole struggle, for all contemporary social evils are "products of the capitalist system".

When the fascists kill a revolutionist, or burn down the building of a proletarian newspaper, the workers are to sigh philosophically: "Alas! Murders and arson are products of the capitalist system", and go home with easy consciences. Fatalist prostration is substituted for the militant theory of Marx, to the sole advantage of the class enemy. The ruin of the petty bourgeoisie is, of course, the product of capitalism. The growth of the fascist bands is, in turn, a product of the ruin of the petty bourgeoisie. But on the other hand, the increase in the misery and the revolt of the proletariat are also products of capitalism, and the militia, in its turn, is the product of the sharpening of the class struggle. Why, then, for the "Marxists" of *l'Humanite*, are the fascist bands the legitimate product of capitalism and the workers' militia the illegitimate product of -- the Trotskyists? It is impossible to make head or tail of this.

"We have to deal with the whole system," we are told.

How? Over the heads of human beings? The fascists in the different countries began with their revolvers and ended by destroying the whole "system" of workers' organizations. How else to check the armed offensive of the enemy if not by an armed defence in order, in our turn, to go over to the offensive.

L'Humanite now admits defence in words, but only in the form of "mass self-defence". The militia is harmful because, you see, it divides the combat detachments from the masses. But why then are there independent armed detachments among the fascists who are not cut off from the reactionary masses but who, on the contrary, arouse the courage and embolden those masses by their well-organized attacks? Or perhaps the proletarian mass is inferior in combative quality to the declassed petty bourgeoisie?

Hopelessly tangled, *l'Humanite* finally begins to hesitate: it appears that mass self-defence requires the creation of special "self-defence groups". In place of the rejected militia, special groups or detachments are proposed. It would seem at first sight that there is a difference only in the name. Certainly, the name proposed by *l'Humanite* means nothing. One can speak of "mass self-defence" but it is impossible to speak of "self-defence groups" since the purpose of the groups is not to defend themselves but the workers' organizations. However, it is not, of course, a question of the name. The "self-defence groups", according to *l'Humanite*, must renounce the use of arms in order not to fall into "putschism". These sages treat the working-class like an infant who must not be allowed to hold a razor in his hands. Razors, moreover, are the monopoly, as we know, of the *Camelots du Roi*[26], who are a legitimate "product of capitalism" and who, with the aid of razors, have overthrown the "system" of democracy. In any case, how are the "self-defence groups" going to defend themselves against the fascist revolvers? "Ideologically", of course. In other words: they can hide themselves. Not having what they require in their hands, they will have to seek "self-defence" in their feet. And the fascists will in the meanwhile sack the workers' organizations with impunity. But if the proletariat suffers a terrible defeat, it will at any rate not have been guilty of "putschism". This fraudulent chatter, parading under the banner of "Bolshevism", arouses only disgust and loathing.

During the "third period" of happy memory -- when the strategists of *l'Humanite* were afflicted with barricade delirium, "conquered" the streets every day and stamped as "social fascist" everyone who did not share their extravagances -- we predicted: "The moment these gentlemen burn the tips of their fingers, they will become the worst opportunists." That prediction has now been completely confirmed. At a time when within the Socialist Party the movement in favor of the militia is growing and strengthening, the leaders of the so-called Communist Party run for the hose to cool down the desire of the advanced workers to organize themselves in fighting columns. Could one imagine a more demoralizing or more damning work than this?

---

[26] French monarchists grouped around Charles Maurras' newspaper, Action Francaise, which was violently anti-democratic.

In the ranks of the Socialist Party sometimes this objection is heard: "A militia must be formed but there is no need of shouting about it."

One can only congratulate comrades who wish to protect the practical side of the business from inquisitive eyes and ears. But it would be much too naive to think that a militia could be created unseen and secretly within four walls. We need tens, and later hundreds, of thousands of fighters. They will come only if millions of men and women workers, and behind them the peasants, understand the necessity for the militia and create around the volunteers an atmosphere of ardent sympathy and active support. Conspiratorial care can and must envelop only the technical aspect of the matter. The political campaign must be openly developed, in meetings, factories, in the streets and on the public squares.

The fundamental cadres of the militia must be the factory workers grouped according to their place of work, known to each other and able to protect their combat detachments against the provocations of enemy agents far more easily and more surely than the most elevated bureaucrats. Conspirative general staffs without an open mobilization of the masses will at the moment of danger remain impotently suspended in midair. Every working-class organization has to plunge into the job. In this question, there can be no line of demarcation between the working-class parties and the trade unions. Hand in hand, they must mobilize the masses. The success of the people militia will then be fully assured.

"But where are the workers going to get arms" object the sober "realists" -- that is to say, frightened philistines -- "the enemy has rifles, cannon, tanks, gas, and airplanes. The workers have a few hundred revolvers and pocket knives."

In this objection, everything is piled up to frighten the workers. On the one hand, our sages identify the arms of the fascists with the armament of the state. On the other hand, they turn towards the state and demand that it disarm the fascists. Remarkable logic! In fact, their position is false in both cases. In France, the fascists are still far from controlling the state. On February 6, they entered in armed conflict with the state police. That is why it is false to speak of cannon and tanks when it is a matter of the immediate armed struggle against the fascists. The fascists, of course, are richer than we. It is easier for them to buy arms. But the workers are more numerous, more determined, more devoted, when they are conscious of a firm revolutionary leadership.

In addition to other sources, the workers can arm themselves at the expense of the fascists by systematically disarming them.

This is now one of the most serious forms of the struggle against fascism. When workers' arsenals will begin to stock up at the expense of the fascist arms depots, the banks and trusts will be more prudent in financing the armament of their murderous guards. It would even be possible in this case -- but in this case only -- that the alarmed authorities would really begin to prevent the arming of the fascists in order not to provide an additional source of arms for the workers. We have known for a long time that only a revolutionary tactic engenders, as a by-product, "reforms" or concessions from the government.

But how to disarm the fascists? Naturally, it is impossible to do so with newspaper articles alone. Fighting squads must be created. An intelligence service must be established. Thousands of informers and friendly helpers will volunteer from all sides when they realize that the business has been seriously undertaken by us. It requires a will to proletarian action.

But the arms of the fascists are, of course, not the only source. In France, there are more than one million organized workers. Generally speaking, this number is small. But it is entirely sufficient to make a beginning in the organization of a workers' militia. If the parties and unions armed only a tenth of their members, that would already be a force of 100,000 men. there is no doubt whatever that the number of volunteers who would come forward on the morrow of a "united front" appeal for a workers' militia would far exceed that number. The contributions of the parties and unions, collections and voluntary subscriptions, would within a month or two make it possible to assure the arming of 100,000 to 200,000 working-class fighters. The fascist rabble would immediately sink its tail between its legs. The whole perspective of development would become incomparably more favorable.

To invoke the absence of arms or other objective reasons to explain why no attempt has been made up to now to create a militia, is to fool oneself and others. The principle obstacle -- one can say the only obstacle -- has its roots in the conservative and passive character of the leaders of the workers' organizations. The skeptics who are the leaders do not believe in the strength of the proletariat. They put their hope in all sorts of miracles from above instead of giving a revolutionary outlet to the energies pulsing below. The socialist workers must compel their leaders to pass over immediately to the creation of the workers' militia or else give way to younger, fresher forces.

A strike is inconceivable without propaganda and without agitation. It is also inconceivable without pickets who, when they can, use persuasion, but when obliged, use force. The strike is the most elementary form of the class struggle which always combines, in varying proportions, "ideological" methods with physical methods. The struggle against fascism is basically a political struggle which needs a militia just as the strike needs pickets. Basically, the picket is the embryo of the workers' militia. He who thinks of renouncing "physical" struggle must renounce all struggle, for the spirit does not live without flesh.

Following the splendid phrase of the great military theoretician Clausewitz, war is the continuation of politics by other means. This definition also fully applies to civil war. It is impermissable to oppose one to the other since it is impossible to check at will the political struggle when it transforms itself, by force of inner necessity, into a political struggle.

The duty of a revolutionary party is to foresee in time the inescapability of the transformation of politics into open armed conflict, and with all its forces to prepare for that moment just as the ruling classes are preparing.

The militia detachments for defence against fascism are the first step on the road to the arming of the proletariat, not the last. Our slogan is:

"Arm the proletariat and the revolutionary peasants!"

The workers' militia must, in the final analysis, embrace all the toilers. To fulfill this program completely would be possible only in a workers' state into whose hands would pass all the means of production and, consequently, also all the means of destruction -- i.e., all the arms and the factories which produce them.

However, it is impossible to arrive at a workers' state with empty hands. Only political invalids like Renaudel[27] can speak of a peaceful, constitutional road to socialism. The constitutional road is cut by trenches held by the fascist bands. There are not a few trenches before us. The bourgeoisie will not hesitate to resort to a dozen coups d'etat. aided by the police and the army, to prevent proletariat from coming to power.

A workers' socialist state can be created only by a victorious revolution.

Every revolution is prepared by the march of economic and political development, but it is always decided by open armed conflicts

---

[27] Pierre Renaudel (1871-1935): Prior to WWI, socialist leader Jean Jaures' righthand man and editor of l'Humanite. During the war, a right-wing social patriot. In the 1930s, he and Marcel Deat led revisionist "neo-socialist" tendency. Voted down at the July 1933 convention, this tendency split from the Socialist Party. After the fascist riots of February 6, 1934, most of the "neos" joined the Radical Party, the main party of French capitalism.

between hostile classes. A revolutionary victory can become possible only as a result of long political agitation, a lengthy period of education and organization of the masses.

But the armed conflict itself must likewise be prepared long in advance.

The advanced workers must know that they will have to fight and win a struggle to the death. They must reach out for arms, as a guarantee of their emancipation.

The Perspective in the United States

The backwardness of the United State working class is only a relative term.[28] In very many important respects, it is the most progressive working class of the world, technically and in its standard of living....

The American workers are very combative -- as we have seen during the strikes. They have had the most rebellious strikes in the world. What the American worker misses is a spirit of generalization, or analysis, of his class position in society as a whole. This lack of social thinking has its origin in the country's whole history....

About fascism

In all the countries where fascism became victorious, we had, before the growth of fascism and its victory, a wave of radicalism of the masses -- of the workers and the poorer peasants and farmers, and of the petty bourgeois class. In Italy, after the war and before 1922, we had a revolutionary wave of tremendous dimensions; the state was paralyzed, the police did not exist, the trade unions could do anything they wanted -- but there was not party capable of taking the power. As a reaction came fascism.

In Germany, the same. We had a revolutionary situation in 1918; the bourgeois class did not even ask to participate in the power. The social democrats paralyzed the revolution. Then the workers tried again in 1922-23-24. This was the time of the bankruptcy of the Communist Party -- all of which we have gone into before. Then in 1929-30-31, the German workers began again a new revolutionary wave. There was a tremendous power in the Communists and in the trade unions, but then came the famous policy (on the part of the Stalinist movement) of social fascism, a policy invented to paralyze the working class. Only after these three tremendous waves did fascism

---

[28] From "Some Questions on American Problems", Fourth International, October 1940

become a big movement. There are no exceptions to this rule -- fascism comes only when the working class shows complete incapacity to take into its own hands the fate of society.

In the United States you will have the same thing. Already, there are fascist elements, and they have, of course, the examples of Italy and Germany. They will, therefore, work in a more rapid tempo. But you also have the examples of other countries. The next historic wave in the United States will be the wave of radicalism of the masses, not fascism. Of course, the war can hinder the radicalization for some time, but then it will give to the radicalization a more tremendous tempo and swing.

We must not identify war dictatorship -- the dictatorship of the military machine, of the staff, of finance capital -- with a fascist dictatorship. For the latter, there is first necessary a feeling of desperation of large masses of the people. When the revolutionary parties betray them, when the vanguard of workers shows it incapacity to lead the people to victory -- then the farmers, the small business men, the unemployed, the soldiers, etc., become capable of supporting a fascist movement, but only then.

A military dictatorship is purely a bureaucratic institution, reinforced by the military machine and based upon the disorientation of the people and their submission to it. After some time their feelings can change and they can become rebellious against the dictatorship.

Build The Revolutionary Party!

In every discussion of political topics the question arises: Shall we succeed in creating a strong party for the moment when the crisis comes? Might not fascism anticipate us? Isn't a fascist stage of development inevitable?

The successes of fascism easily make people lose all perspective, lead them to forget the actual conditions which made the strengthening and the victory of fascism possible. Yet a clear understanding of these conditions is of especial importance to the workers of he United States. We may set it down as a historical law: fascism was able to conquer only in those countries where the conservative labour parties prevented the proletariat from utilizing the revolutionary situation and seizing power. In Germany two revolutionary situations were involved: 1918-1919 and 1923-1924. Even in 1929, a direct struggle for power on the part of the proletariat was still possible. In all these three cases, the social democracy and the Comintern [the Stalinists] criminally and viciously disrupted the conquest of power and thereby placed society in an impasse. Only under these conditions and in this situation did the stormy rise of fascism and its gaining of power prove possible.

* * *

Insofar as the proletariat proves incapable, at a given stage, of conquering power, imperialism begins regulating economic life with its own methods; the fascist party which becomes the state power is the political mechanism. The productive forces are in irreconcilable contradiction not only with private property but also with national state boundaries. Imperialism is the very expression of this contradiction. Imperialist capitalism seeks to solve this contradiction through an extension of boundaries, seizure of new territories, and so on. The totalitarian state, subjecting all aspects of economic, political, and cultural life to finance capital, is the instrument for creating a supernationalist state, an imperialist empire, the rule over continents, the rule over the whole world.

All these traits of freedom we have analyzed, each one by itself and all of them in their totality, to the extent that they became manifest or came to the forefront.

Both theoretical analysis as well as the rich historical experience of the last quarter of a century have demonstrated with equal force that fascism is each time the final link of a specific political cycle composed of the following: the gravest crisis of capitalist society; the growth of the radicalization of the working class; the growth of sympathy toward the working class, and a yearning for change on the part of the rural and urban petty bourgeoisie; the extreme confusion of the big bourgeoisie; its cowardly and treacherous manoeuvres aimed at avoiding the revolutionary climax; the exhaustion of the proletariat; growing confusion and indifference; the aggravation of the social crisis; the despair of the petty bourgeoisie, its yearning for change; the collective neurosis of the petty bourgeoisie, its readiness to believe in miracles, its readiness for violent measures; the growth of hostility towards the proletariat, which has deceived its expectations. These are the premises for a swift formation of a fascist party and its victory.

It is quite self-evident that the radicalization of the working class in the United States has passed through only its initial phases, almost exclusively, in the sphere of the trade union movement (the CIO). The prewar period, and then the war itself, may temporarily interrupt this process of radicalization, especially if a considerable number of workers are absorbed into war industry. But this interruption of the process of radicalization cannot be of a long duration. The second stage of radicalization will assume a more sharply expressive character. The problem of forming an independent labour party will be put on the order of the day. Our transitional demands will gain great

50

popularity. On the other hand, the fascist, reactionary tendencies will withdraw to the background, assuming a defensive position, awaiting a more favorable moment. This is the nearest perspective. No occupation is more completely unworthy than that of speculating whether or not we shall succeed in creating a powerful revolutionary leader-party. Ahead lies a favorable perspective, providing all the justification for revolutionary activism. It is necessary to utilize the opportunities which are opening up and to build the revolutionary party.

The Events in Germany
Maurice Spector

All who resisted have been shot, some have committed suicide. Without the ceremony even of a drumhead court martial, the souls of Roehm and his staff were dispatched to Valhalla amid farewell accusations of sodomy. Partisans of due process of law protest that there was no evidence of overt conspiracy, that Hitler's Reichstag oration was "an accounting without vouchers" by one who was prosecuting attorney, witness, judge and executioner. But conspiracies, like convenient "assassinations", can always be invented.[29]

What Hitler-Goering-Goebbels faced was the much more deadly fact of a condition. In the historic social crisis of a falling rate of profit and mounting class antagonisms, Capital had decided that the only alternative to socialization was the forcible degradation of wages to the barest level of subsistence. The end entailed the complete destruction of all the barriers of proletarian organization; its instrumentality was the "anti-Marxist" mobilization of the petty-bourgeoisie, a victim itself of monopolist expropriation. The working class, criminally divided and betrayed, virtually capitulated without a struggle; the trade unions, the social democracy, and the communists were crushed.

Intoxicated by its easy triumph, the middle class mistakes the illusion of power for its substance; it attempts to function as an independent social force. At this point, the reality of Fascism clashes with its demagogic form. The Jacobin petty-bourgeoisie, which saved a great revolution from feudal reaction, had finally to cede command of the state to Big Business. The Brown shirt creatures of the capitalist twilight could not succeed where the Red Bonnets of the capitalist dawn had failed. The plebeian phase of German Fascism is liquidated.

The blood-purge of the Storm Troops was a preventive coup d'etat against the elements of the "second revolution". Stripped of its nebulous flights into ethics and metaphysics, von Papen's Marburg address was the unmistakeable handwriting on the wall. This hero of the Herrenklub, by the side of whom Judas Iscariot was positively a saint, knew first-hand as intermediary between embezzling Junkers

---

[29] From New International, Vol.1 No.2, August 1934, pp.47-48. Maurice Spector (1898 - August 1, 1968) was the Chairman of the Communist Party of Canada for much of the 1920s and an early follower of Leon Trotsky after his explusion from the Communist International in 1927.

and Ruhr industrialists, that Hitler was a product of capitalist subsidy no less than of middle class misery.

Had Marxism been suppressed, he now asked, so that national Bolshevism would be instituted in its place? It was plainly necessary that the Fighting League of the Trading Middle Classes and its military counterpart, the SA be taught the limits of the totalitarian state. Hitler preferred to be the agent rather than the victim of this necessity.

When in 1926 he declared the Nazi program "unalterable", Hitler intended by that no more than his Italian prototype who at a similar stage favored the abolition of the monarchy, the dissolution of joint stock corporations, and transfer of large estates to the peasants' cooperatives. Once the March on Rome was accomplished (a single regiment of regulars could have dispersed it) and the Facta government had by secret agreement delivered over the power, Mussolini set about trampling down all in his own party who had taken his demagogy at its face value. Except for the brutal reality of the Fascist syndicates, the "corporate state" remains a petty-bourgeois fantasy on paper. So, too, Hitler came not to destroy German capitalism but to fulfill neo-German imperialism. The program of nationalization of the trusts, confiscation of the land, and abolition of "interest-servitude" was like the whole propaganda of anti-Semitism designed as bait for the lower middle class. The Aryan capital of the Krupps, Thyssen and Siemens was pronounced "creative" and sacrosanct. The autarchy which Hitler advocated is to be understood in the context of his published view that the "mere restoration of the German frontiers of 1914 is a political lunacy and a crime".

The Alfred Rosenbergs are no less aware than any Marxist that the productive forces have outgrown the boundaries of the national state, that Ruhr coal cannot be permanently divorced from Lorraine iron-ore without dire consequences for German economy. A scientific anthropologist like Boas misses the point that the Nordic racial ideology is the Nazi pseudonym for the new imperialism.

In this light, those who have profited from the Hitler regime are easily distinguished. There are first the Junkers whose estates despite the "unalterable program" remain intact and who have been accorded higher tariffs. The industrialists who invested so heavily in Hitler have received about one billion dollars worth of returns in the form of tax reductions, subsidies and wage cuts. The upper middle class, the social base of the black-shirted Schutzstaffel (the SS), has profited from openings created by the ostracism of Jews and liberal office-holders of the Weimar regime. But the lower middle classes, dazzled with the heralded prosperity of the Third Reich; have been given a stone, the processes of rationalization and centralization continue their grind.

The economic crisis grows acute. An increasingly unfavorable trade balance with shrinking reserves of gold and foreign exchange foster projects for the devaluation of the mark and a moratorium of foreign payments. Except for the heavily subsidized armament industries, unemployment has not decreased; it is merely concealed. Real wages have sunk to their lowest level in half a century. Expenditures on the social services have been cut by nearly half a billion marks. Such soil could not but nourish hopes of a "second revolution" to bring the Nazi masses into their own. Man does not live by bread alone but the most immaculately conceived Aryan and lineal descendant of Hermann the Cheruscan cannot live on glory alone.

Captain Roehm and his circle of military desperadoes had but small interest in the National-Bolshevist ideas of a Strasser, but they were prepared to utilize the disaffection of the petty bourgeois masses as their base of operations for the control of the Reichswehr. The command of the Reichswehr, on the other hand, was quite as resolved as had been the Royal Italian Army to allow no parvenu weakening of its monopoly or plebeian dilution of the ranks by fusion with the SA.

The military question involved the whole complex of political and economic orientation. Hitler always viewed the Storm Troops with distrust as a menace to his exclusive control of the party. He had been dangerously embroiled with them at the time of the Berlin mutiny of Captain Stennes, which only the treacherous services of Goebbels helped him put down. The proposed reduction of the Storm Troop numbers aimed a direct and telling blow at the plans and ambitions of Roehm. In killing him, Hitler disposed of one of the most influential of Nazi originals and its ablest military organizer. The simultaneous killing of von Schleicher bears the familiar earmarks of the "amalgam".

Any contact the "social" General may have had with Roehm would have been quite casual; their respective points of support and perspectives were fundamentally dissimilar. But the murder of von Schleicher, removed as it were, a "Bonapartist" pretender, and cushioned the shock of annihilating so many Nazis. The death of von Hindenburg and Hitler's assumption of the added presidential powers, completes the concentration of all sovereignty, of every organ of legislative and executive authority in the hands of finance capital. Having settled accounts with the turbulent petty bourgeoisie, its pawn against the proletariat, Fascism now assumes the form of a bureaucratic military and police dictatorship.

The working class did not intervene. Wedding, formerly the reddest district of Berlin, was deserted. That is the tragic measure of the catastrophe of 1933. Only that department of the Stalin press dedicated to sowing apocalyptic illusions represented Germany as on the verge of a proletarian revolution. A truer index of Stalin's appraisal of the situation is Litvinov's Realpolitik, his adoption of the French imperialist thesis of "security before disarmament" and endless regional pacts.

A direct transition from Fascist dictatorship to Soviet power is theoretically not inconceivable. But the pre-requisite for that would have to be the lever of a powerful communist party. None such is available. The Stalinist party, which, planless and headless, capitulated without struggle when Hitler ascended to the Chancellery, is scarcely recognizable in the panegyrics and embellishments of the official and semi-official Comintern propagandists. A party which cannot distinguish victory from defeat, is of no greater actual service to the proletariat than a party which directly betrays it.

But while in the circumstances there could be no revolutionary intervention of the working class, conditions have been created for its infusion with fresh confidence. The change in the relations of the petty bourgeoisie to monopoly capital as the lessons of the blood-purge seep in, must inevitably draw the middle classes closer to the proletariat. If only the latter displays the necessary revolutionary clearsightedness a change in the balance of forces will follow.

It was the inability of the proletariat to solve the social crisis, and the failure of its parties to give decisive leadership that alienated the petty bourgeoisie, sending it into the camp of capital. The greatest step forward that the German proletariat could take today and the guarantee so far as that is possible of its victory tomorrow would be to digest the lessons of its own defeat of 1933 and from that to form the cadres of the party of the Fourth International.

How It Happened in Italy

The longer German Fascism prevails, the more it reveals at every important stage of its development an essential resemblance to its Italian precursor. The analogy is so striking in all important aspects that it is now possible to record a set of evolutionary laws ruling the life's span of Fascism. If in external manifestations the German development takes on more convulsive and sensational forms, and are more concentrated in point of time, this general accentuation does not invalidate the comparison with Italy. It only indicates that the unfolding of the Nazi movement is taking place in a country where class formations and antagonisms are sharper and more clear-cut, where the social and economic structure is far more developed, and where the foreign political situation is vastly more complicated and critical.[30]

Fascism differs from every other form of capitalist dictatorship in that it commences as a vast popular movement of a middle class turned desperately reactionary. Its essential nature as an instrument of finance capital brings it inexorably to the point where this broad social foundation, having served its purpose in eliminating the working class as an organized political factor, is itself likewise eliminated.

The recent events in Germany make this ineluctable trend dramatically apparent. Were moral depravity and military ambition the only sins of Captain Roehm, neither he nor his coadjutors would have been dispatched to join their ancestors. After all, the homosexual predilections and military talent of Friedrich II never aroused much indignation in his time, either. The social offense of the Roehms and Strassers in the eyes of the real ruling class in Germany, was their insistence upon playing too long with the thoroughly inconvenient aspirations of the parvenu middle class. The attempt to dilute the compact Reichswehr with Storm Trooper-, symbol of the whole program of a middle class imperiously demanding payment on the promissory notes of Fascist demagoguery, was given the only reply which real, and not apparent, class relations had prepared for it.

The first Fascia Italiano di Combattimento was formed by Mussolini in Milan in March 1919 and was very quickly duplicated in all the principal centers of northern Italy. "These Fasci by no means had a reactionary character, they appeared much rather as a

---

[30] From New International, Vol.1 No.2, August 1934, pp.48-49, where it was signed I.C.H.

subversive 'revolutionary' movement", on whose banner was inscribed the "struggle for the revolutionary fruits of the revolutionary war". The first regular Fascist congress adopted a platform remarkable in its middle class radicalism. Women's suffrage, the lowering of the voting age, proportional representation, the abolition of the Senate, an economic parliament by the side of the political, a national assembly to consider constitutional reform, legislative guarantee of an eight-hour day, minimum wage for all workers, invalid and old-age insurance, a form of workers' control of production, a steep and progressive income tax tantamount to outright confiscation in many cases, confiscation of war profits up to 85%, the confiscation of clerical wealth, the abolition of the standing army and the establishment of a defensive people's militia with short-term training periods, nationalization of all arms and munitions plants – these were the outstanding planks in the original Fascist platform. They enabled it to rally not only wide strata of the middle class but many workers as well.

The fact that big agrarians and industrialists guided and financed the Fascists in their murderous assaults upon every labour organization and institution, that following Facta's resignation Mussolini was asked by the king to form a cabinet only after the telegraphic demand of the Confederazione Generale dell'Industria, is quite well known. Not less contestable, however, is the equally important fact that hundreds of thousands of middle class and proletarian masses looked to Fascism in power for an amelioration if not a solution of their lot. They were quickly undeceived.

The promised proportional representation in elections not only was not introduced, but even the mild form of it established in 1919 was abolished and its place taken at first by an outrageously inequitable "majority system" aimed at drastically reducing the representation of the non-Fascist parties. The woman's suffrage put into effect was so circumscribed that it was actually confined to the members of the upper classes. Senate and constitution remained without modification in the direction originally indicated. The eight-hour day was "guaranteed" in such a way that the exception became the rule. Wages were reduced to such a point that the League of Nations could recently register Italy at the bottom of the European list. Pensions and insurance were practically abolished.

Instead of control of production by the workers, the factory councils were suppressed. Taxation took a course directly opposed to the old pledges. Luxury, automobile and inheritance taxes were completely abolished; a tax on wages was introduced, and indirect taxation assumed monstrous dimensions. The clergy's wealth remained undisturbed, but religious instruction in the schools, voluntary in Italy for fifty years, was reestablished. Military service was increased from eight to eighteen months; instead of the popular militia, a Fascist Praetorian Guard of half a million men was organized; veterans' pensions were reduced while vast subsidies were granted war industries and big orders placed for cannon and airplanes.

The proletarian, and above all the petty bourgeois, rubbed his eyes in rueful bitterness and astonishment at the reality of the first year of Fascist sovereignty. The fruits of their revolution were not for them. A tardy disillusionment set in.

"I was an apostle of the first program of the Fascists," read an open letter written to Mussolini in 1923 by Edoardo Frosini, one of the "Fascists of the first hour" who presided over the first Fascist congress.

"At that time there were not yet any Blackshirts. You, however, still wore our insignia: a red cockade over the tricolor ... With the passage of time you altered the program of 1919 in such a manner that you are protecting those whom original Fascism promised primarily to combat. You have flung yourself into the arms of those whom you wanted to crush and Fascism has become synonymous with reaction in the service of the bourgeoisie and the monarchy ..."

And how like the latter-day insurgent Nazis just put to death by Hitler does it sound when one reads an eleven-year-old article by Farinacci about the "small clique which keeps Mussolini under its spell"; or the speeches of the Fascist under-secretary of state, De Vecchi and the deputy Albanese who openly attacked the government; or the declaration of Cesare Forni in favor of the "second march on Rome" – the equivalent in those days of the "second revolution" in contemporary Nazi Germany. All that has happened there in the last three months is like a thunderous echo of the events in Italy a decade ago!

The petty bourgeoisie clamored for the fulfillment of the alluring promises that had fascinated them from 1919 to 1922. And open civil war broke out in the Fascist party. No city but witnessed a crisis, easily as severe as the Bavarian boudoir interlude of Roehm and Hitler. In Rome, the two contending factions into which the party was split twice marched against each other with bombs and machine guns, and a violent collision was averted only by the intercession of the most prominent party personalities. In Leghorn the dissidents broke into the Fascist militia's barracks, seized banners and trophies and then occupied the party headquarters. In Turin, Genoa and elsewhere fighting took place between the rival Fascist groups. In Savona, the opposition occupied the city hall, the sub-prefecture, the headquarters of the party and the trade unions. As late as 1926, Trieste witnessed two days of street fighting and a state of siege had to be proclaimed; in Rome an attempt was made to seize police headquarters.

Even if less spectacularly than in Germany, the bourgeoisie clubbed the duped middle classes into submission with no less energy and resolution. The "constructive period" of Fascism, said Mussolini a few months after the march on Rome, requires different methods than the "destructive period" – which meant that the petty bourgeoisie had been useful in destroying the labour movement but was now superfluous and even dangerous.

"Since certain sporadic episodes of recent date, which are to be characterized as entirely unjustified acts of violence, give grounds to fear that there are still some elements who have not quite grasped the new situation of Fascism," warned Mussolini's personal organ, Popolo d'Italia, less than a year after his triumph, "we have reason to believe that the government is determined to enjoin an absolute respect of the laws upon all – especially also upon the leaders and soldiers of Fascism ... Every disturber of the peace is an enemy, even if he carries a membership book of the Fascist party in his pocket."

The dictator himself declared in the *Corriero Italiano* in September 1923:

"Should we be unable radically to rejuvenate the Fascist party, then it would be better to destroy it and to permit the healthy and fresh forces which live and work within it to merge powerfully into the freer and broader national stream."[31]

As with the Reichswehr, the attempt to pack the Italian army with Fascist upstarts was a complete failure. The original plan, directed by General Di Giorgio, was to clear the garrisons, send regiments to the frontiers, and fill their places, above all in the large cities, with Fascist battalions. But almost to a man the army generals led by Marshal Cadorna, speedily defeated the plan. And if Di Giorgio did not meet the same fate as Captain Roehm, he was nevertheless sacrificed by

---

[31] Compare this with the following excerpts:

"The Berlin NSBO numbers more than 400,000 members today; we shall now slowly have to take inventory. Perhaps we shall have to throw out some 80 to 100 thousand. But better a quarter of a million fighters who know why they are fighting and what they're here for, than a half a million who are nothing but a wild mob." (Herr Goebbel's Angriff, May 22, 1933.)

"Instead of these newly accepted members seeing their task in working and proving their worth to the party, they who in past years never thought of being radical, they want to outbid us in radicalism. So they come with the party program and the Hitler book, Mein Kampf, and ask: Why isn't this carried out yet? Why aren't the banks socialized yet? And they think they can impress us by that." (Herr Goebbels, *Vossische Zeitung*, May 20, 1933.)

Mussolini, who promised the high command that no reform of the army would be undertaken without consulting the military.

The party itself was beaten to an amorphous, voiceless pulp. Mussolini first had to suspend provincial congresses by telegram for fear of the opposition. Later, the elective principle was abolished. Mussolini took over the power to appoint the general secretary of the party, who in turn appointed the provincial secretaries, who thereupon appointed the local secretaries. Both national and provincial party congresses were completely abolished, and party policy became the exclusive prerogative of the Grand Fascist Council appointed by Il Duce. "The slogan is," Mussolini made it clear in 1926, when the last remnant of active middle class and proletarian opposition was driven under ground, "absolute submission!"

The comparison holds even down to the detail of Der Führer dropping his pilots. "The revolution devours its children." Of the "Fascists of the first hour", there are few who did not meet with essentially as cruel a fate as Hitler's early cronies. The "extremist" Farinacci, replaced as general party secretary by Augusto Turati, met with disgrace in 1926 when it was revealed that he had blackmailed support for his personal organ, Il Regime Fascista, from the wealthy and that he had been mixed up in the financial scandals surrounding the collapse of his friend Count Lusignani's Agrarian Bank of Parma. Cesare Rossi, the former press chief – the Goebbels of Mussolini – went into exile, as did the deputies Massimo Rocca, Carlo Bazzi and others. The head of the Fascist federation of Rome, Calza Bini, was imprisoned; so was Mussolini's confidante, Amerigo Dumini, the assassin of Matteotti. The notorious Italo Balbo, who murdered the priest Minzoni and invented the castor oil treatment of anti-Fascists, was sent off to Libya. Filippini, who had been disbarred from the practise of law in Milan for his swindles, is not heard of today. Another of the Fascist "originals", Umberto Pasella, was eliminated even earlier. Libero Tancredi, who took women, boys, politics and his comrades' money with equal light-mindedness, also disappeared from the Fascist horizon.

Fascism and Big Business
Daniel Guérin

A particularly dangerous illusion consists in regarding fascism, despite the horror it inspires, as a progressive political phenomenon – as a passing and even necessary, though painful, stage.[32] Rash prophets have announced 10 times, 100 times, the imminent and inevitable crumbling of the fascist dictatorship in Italy or Germany under the blows of the victorious revolution. They have asserted that fascism, by driving class antagonisms to their highest degree of tension, is hastening the hour of the proletarian revolution, even going so far as to contend that the proletariat could conquer power only by passing through the hell of the fascist dictatorship. Today it is no longer possible to keep up such illusions. Events have demonstrated with tragic clearness that the moment the working class allows the fascist wave to sweep over it, a long period of slavery and impotence begins – a long period during which socialist, even democratic, ideas are not merely erased from the pediments of public monuments and libraries but, what is much more serious, are rooted out of human minds. Events have proved that fascism physically destroys everything opposing its dictatorship, no matter how mildly, and that it creates a vacuum around itself and leaves a vacuum behind it.

This extraordinary power to survive by annihilating everything except itself, to hold out against everything and everybody, to hold out for years in spite of internal contradictions and in spite of the misery and discontent of the masses – what is behind it?

Excessive Centralization

The strength of the dictatorship rests first of all in its excessive centralization. Such a regime cannot "by its very nature endure the slightest trace of federalism or autonomy. Like the Convention, like Napoleon, it must seek complete centralism, the logical consequence of its system and the necessary means to insure its permanence." Mussolini and Hitler strengthen to the utmost the authority of the

---

[32] Daniel Guérin (19 May 1904, Paris – 14 April 1988) was a French author, In the 1930s he was one of the leaders of the Parti Socialiste Ouvrier et Paysan (PSOP - "Workers and Peasants Socialist Party"), and was at that time quite close to Leon Trotsky. In 1933, he traveled to Nazi Germany, an experience which inspired him to author Fascism and Big Business, in which he detailed the roots of nazi ideology and its ties to capitalism. Gradually, his ethos edged into a combination of Marxism and anarchism

central government and suppress even the faintest trace of individualism. In Italy the powers of the provincial governors have been considerably increased.

"It must be clear," a communication from the Duce informs them, "that authority cannot be divided ... Authority is single and unified. If it were not, we should fall back into a disorganized state."

In Germany the seventeen "states", whose rights to their own governments and parliaments were preserved by the Weimar Constitution, have been gradually suppressed and transformed into mere provinces of the Reich, directly administered by representatives of the central government, the Statthalter. Extolling his centralizing work, Hitler boasts of having "given the people the Constitution that will make them strong".

Marx in his time was able to rejoice because the executive power, while becoming ever more concentrated, simultaneously concentrated against itself all the forces of destruction. And certain of our contemporaries, with a somewhat too simple conception of the dialectic, imagine that by centralizing to the utmost, fascism is working automatically for the Revolution. They would be correct if fascism did not, at the same time as it centralizes, destroy in the most radical fashion the "forces of destruction" themselves.

Fascism, in fact, has brought to the highest degree of perfection the methods of police repression used in modern states. It has made the political police a truly scientific organization. The Italian Ovra, the German Gestapo – real "states within the state", with ramifications in all classes of society and even in every dwelling house, with enormous financial and material resources, and with limitless powers – are in a position literally to annihilate at birth every attempt at opposition wherever it appears. They can arrest at any time, "put away" on a remote island or in a concentration camp, even execute without a semblance of a trial, anyone they wish. Consequently it is possible to say that such a regime is a smooth block of granite where no hand can find a hold. Gentizon is not far from the truth, unfortunately, when he says of Italy: "Opposition has completely disappeared ... With the system of the totalitarian state, no hostile propaganda is possible."

And Goebbels too when he asserts: "The enemies of the regime are completely put down; there is no longer in the whole country any opposition worthy of the name."

Dispersal of the Working Class
Added to these methods of police repression is the state of "forced disunity, dispersion and helplessness" in which fascism keeps the working class. Certainly in neither Italy nor Germany can the regime

boast of having all the proletariat with it; quite the contrary. Mussolini himself is forced to confess:

"I cannot say that I have [with me] all the workers ... They are perpetual malcontents."

In Germany, the elections to the factory "confidential councils" have twice (April, 1934, and April, 1935) constituted a stinging defeat for the regime. According to the later admission of Dr. Ley himself, scarcely 40 per cent of the electors voted in 1934. In 1935 at least 30 per cent of the electors abstained or voted against. In 1936, 1937, and 1938 the elections were "postponed" as a precautionary measure, and in June, 1938, it was decided that the "confidential men" would no longer be "elected" but appointed by the head of the company.

This latent discontent, however, finds it almost impossible to express itself or to organize. The working class is atomized and disintegrated. It is true that protest movements have appeared here and there, but they are stifled immediately. They are restricted to isolated plants and known to few workers outside the plants where they occur; in each factory the workers believe they are alone in their resistance. Not only are the ties broken between the workers in different factories, but even inside large enterprises contacts no longer exist between the employees of the various departments, and it is very difficult to re-establish them. Even when the embryos of illegal unions are formed, with heroic efforts, they are almost always crushed in the egg.

No doubt there are militant socialists and communists who distribute illegal leaflets at the peril of their lives, but they are only an heroic and constantly decimated phalanx. The workers lose their passivity only when an event abroad reveals to them that they are not alone, that beyond the frontiers other workers are struggling. Thus the great strikes of June, 1936, in France, in spite of the care of the fascist press to minimize their importance, had a profound echo among the workers of Italy and Germany.[33]

Fascist Education

And while fascism puts its adult opponents in a position where they can do no harm, it imposes its imprint on the young and shapes

---

[33] On April 18, 1937. Rudolf Hess made a violent anti-communist speech at Karlsruhe, which the Berlin correspondent of Information commented on as follows:

"Inside Germany this speech tends to put a stop to the discussions which have arisen among the popular masses of the Reich, despite the censorship, as a result of the promulgation of the forty-hour law and new social laws by the Blum cabinet."

them in its own mold. "The generation of the irre-concilables will be eliminated by natural laws," Mussolini exults. "Soon the younger generation will come!" Volpe speaks lustingly of this "virgin material which has not yet been touched by the old ideologies."

"Our future is represented by the German youth," Hitler declares. "We will raise it in our own spirit. If the older generation cannot become accustomed to it, we will take their children from them. ..."

"We want to inculcate our principles in the children from their most tender years."

And Goebbels asserts that as long as the youth are behind Hitler, the regime will be indestructible. At the age of four in Germany and at six in Italy, the child is taken from his family, enrolled in the militarized formations of fascism, and subjected to an intensive stuffing with propaganda. The dictatorial state puts in his hands a single newspaper, a single textbook, and educates him in an incredible atmosphere of exaltation and fanaticism.

This training accomplishes its aim. Although the regime in Germany has not been in power long enough to enable us to formulate valid conclusions, in Italy the results are tangible: "The youth can no longer even conceive of socialist or communist ideas," Gentizon writes. A militant worker, Feroci, confirms this:

"A youth that has never read a labour paper, never attended a labour meeting, and knows nothing of socialism and communism ... that is ... what makes for the real strength of Mussolini's regime."

Doubtless there is something fascist education cannot stifle, and which does not need to be taught – the class instinct. No amount of propaganda will ever prevent the young worker from feeling he is exploited. Pietro Nenni, while far from claiming that the Black Shirt youth has already succeeded in freeing itself from the fascist grip, states that in Italy "many young people are socialists without knowing it and without wanting to be." Il Maglio, the weekly paper of the fascist unionists of Turin, complains that among the youth there is a certain lack of understanding of fascist "unionism":

"It is natural that there should be a few young people who, while recognizing that the abolition of all forms of class struggle is an absolute necessity ... still believe that labour's material interests can be better assured by strikes and the methods of struggle used up to yesterday in labour conflicts ..."

In Germany as well, countless young people who believed literally that the Third Reich would be their state, and whom the Third Reich has condemned to forced labour, are bitterly disappointed. But it is extremely difficult for the youth in either country, in view of the mental training they are given, to get rid of the false ideas with which they are indoctrinated, to clarify their revolt, and without guidance do for themselves the work of a century of socialist action and thought. The confused awakening of their class consciousness leads some of them to the "left wing" of fascism or National Socialism; it does not make them into militant revolutionists.

Another illusion about the duration of fascism must be dispelled. Certain people try to deduce from the economic and political contradictions which have developed in the fascist regime that the days of the dictatorship are numbered. These contradictions do exist, and we have analyzed them. They are important enough possibly to bring about profound changes in the structure of the regime. But such changes can occur without the dictatorship itself collapsing.

Dissatisfaction of Big Business

A few supplementary explanations are necessary here. The fact is undeniable that the industrialists who subsidized and put fascism in power are not entirely satisfied with their own creation. In the first place the regime is terribly expensive. The maintenance of the excessive bureaucracy of the state, the party and the numerous semi-governmental bodies costs unheard-of sums and adds to the financial difficulties of the government. In their memorandum of June, 1937, to Hitler, the industrialists wrote:

"It used to be estimated that there was one functionary for every twelve persons in productive occupations. Today, if the official party organizations and the semi-official and corporative services with their functionaries and employees are included, it is estimated that there is one person on the state payroll for every eight persons in productive occupations."

Abandoning any attempt to "estimate the amount of personal and material expenses required by the administrative machine," the authors of the memorandum complained of the "incalculable losses arising from a lack of contact between the old and the new authorities, and the overlapping of functions between the old and new state services and the party."[34] They wished the day would come when "in accordance with a definite principle, a final organization of the internal political apparatus of the state will be possible ..."

While the state must carry huge incidental expenses, the big capitalists themselves have to stand a certain number: "voluntary

[34] "All the chief administrative bodies of the state," the Berlin correspondent of the Temps had observed, "are duplicated, so to speak, by the organs of the National Socialist Party ... The party penetrates into the Ministries, but it also preserves, on the fringes of the traditional administrative bodies, its own organs ..."

contributions" extorted by the party and its "welfare" undertakings; various subscriptions; "graft" and seats on the boards of directors of big companies for the "upper crust" of the fascist leaders, etc. But these incidental expenses, the importance of which must not be exaggerated, are less annoying to big business than the demagogic agitation indulged in by the fascist plebeians – agitation which, despite purges and repressions, periodically reappears, though within constantly narrower limits.

Again, while big business approves of an aggressive policy that brings it new armament orders, it is afraid lest the fascist leaders, in seeking a diversion from the wretchedness of the people, provoke a premature war which will result in the isolation of the country and its defeat. It is especially significant that in the autumn of 1935 it was the fascist leaders, Farinacci, Rossoni, and others, who urged Mussolini into conflict with England, while the big bourgeoisie, the General Staff, and the Crown, on the other hand, advised moderation and caution. Likewise in Germany, when Hitler decided in March, 1936, to remilitarize the Rhineland, it was the Nazi top bureaucracy – Goering, Goebbels, and others – who urged him on to the adventure, while the big capitalists and their representative, Dr. Schacht, as well as the Reichswehr Generals, were wary, not as to the act itself but as to the rash form it took. At the end of December of the same year, General von Fritsch pointed out that neither the Reich nor the German army could undertake any action that might lead to war in a short time, and he went so far as to threaten to resign his command if his expert advice was disregarded.

The Cult of the Leader
Neither does big business look without a certain amount of anxiety on the symptoms of "delusions of grandeur" displayed ever more obviously by the dictator. This development is really inevitable, for in proportion as the plebeians are eliminated and the party relegated to a secondary position, it is necessary to inflate the "Man of Destiny" all the more in order to conceal behind his person the real nature of the fascist state: a military and police dictatorship in the service of big business. It is necessary to follow Spengler's advice:

"Nothing has meaning any more but the purely personal power exercised by the Caesar [in whom] the omnipotence of money disappears."

Thus in Italy, the dictatorship of the fascist party has gradually given place to the personal dictatorship of the Duce. In Germany, during the last electoral campaign, "there [was] very little question of National Socialism and much – to the exclusion of almost everything else – of Herr Hitler." But the dictator himself is taken in by this "booby-trap". The same mishap befalls him as befell Louis Bonaparte:

"Only ... when he himself now takes his imperial role seriously ... does he become the victim of his own conception of the world, the serious buffoon, who no longer takes world history for a comedy but his comedy for world history."

Mussolini and Hitler end by literally becoming egomaniacs. And the big capitalists must increasingly reckon with the boundless pride, the changing humor and whims, of the Duce or the Führer. This means a loss of time and has certain drawbacks.

And finally, the economic policy of fascism, however favorable to themselves it may be, is not entirely satisfactory to the big capitalists. Although they eagerly pocket the fabulous profits from armament orders, they are terrified at the possible consequences of this policy. They are haunted by the thought of a financial catastrophe. They likewise complain, as we have seen, that the "war economy" regime is constantly imposing on them more burdensome state regulations, that it is forever eating away at sacrosanct "private initiative".

Therefore the industrialists are not wholly content, and in the minds of some of them the idea begins to germinate of throwing overboard once and for all the fascist plebeians and their leader himself, and of completing the already far-advanced transformation of the fascist totalitarian regime into a purely military dictatorship.

But they hesitate. They dare not deprive themselves entirely of the incomparable and irreplaceable means of penetrating into all cells of society which they have in the fascist mass organizations. Above all, they hesitate to deprive themselves of the services of the "Man of Destiny", for the mystic faith in the Duce or the Führer, though declining, is not yet extinct.

"The present order in Germany," the Temps states, "exists and continues only thanks to the popularity of the Chancellor and the faith of the German masses in Herr Hitler's actions ..."

"The Führer is unquestionably more popular than the regime."

The "Man of Destiny", however much a nuisance he may be, is still necessary. Even his madness is useful; he alone can still perform the psychological miracle of turning the discontent and wretchedness of large strata of the people into enthusiasm and faith.

But most of all, the industrialists are apprehensive lest a radical change in the regime, such as they desire, should cost much bloodshed. They dread a civil war, even a short one, in which "national" forces would oppose one another; they fear nothing so much as what in Germany is called, in anticipation, a "new June 30". Hence they hesitate.

The hypothesis is not absolutely excluded that some day they will come to feel that the advantages of a purely military dictatorship outweigh its shortcomings. But a change of this nature would not necessarily open up the way to a revolution. It is true that for the middle classes, suddenly deprived of their daily mythology, the awakening would be a cruel one, and that it would be harder, with only the aid of a military and police apparatus, to keep the proletariat enslaved. Yet the authoritarian state, strongly supported by bayonets, might still endure for a time in this new form; it might find new "mysticisms" (the nationalist mysticism, the dynastic mysticism, etc.) to keep large strata of the population under the spell; in a word, even without Mussolini or Hitler, the "strong state" might survive.

If fascism is not progressive politically, it is no more so economically – notwithstanding what certain people think. Stripped of all appearances, all the contradictions which dim its real face, all the secondary aspects which hide from so many its essential character, and all the circumstances peculiar to any one country, fascism is reduced to this: a strong state intended to prolong artificially an economic system based on profit and the private ownership of the means of production. To use the picturesque figure of Radek, fascist dictatorship is the iron hoop with which the bourgeoisie tries to patch up the broken barrel of capitalism. Here some clarification, however, is necessary: the "barrel", contrary to what many believe, was not broken by the revolutionary action of the working class; fascism is not the "bourgeoisie's answer to an attack by the proletariat" but rather "an expression of the decay of capitalist economy". The barrel fell apart of its own accord.

Fascism is, to be sure, a defensive reaction of the bourgeoisie, but a defence against the disintegration of its own system far more than against any proletarian offensive – alas, non-existent. The crisis of the capitalist system itself is what shook capitalism to its foundations by drying up the sources of profit. The working class, on the other hand, paralyzed by its organizations and its leaders in the hour of the decay of capitalist economy, did not know how to take power and replace dying capitalism with socialism.

Capitalism in Decay

As to the nature of this crisis, fascism itself has no illusions.

"The crisis," Mussolini admits, "has penetrated the system so deeply that it has become a systemic crisis. It is no longer a wound, but a chronic disease ..."

In spite of the fact that fascism demagogically promises the reabsorption of unemployment and the resumption of business, it

68

knows perfectly well that it will not set the economic machine going again. It does not seek seriously either to bring back to life the vanished consumer, or to stimulate the long interrupted investment of private savings in production. Others are free to cherish Utopias if they wish, but fascism knows what it wants and what it can do. It merely tries to check, through artificial means, the fall in the profits of a private capitalism which has become parasitic. In spite of its verbose demagogy, it has no great designs; it lives from week to week; it aspires to nothing more than to keep alive – through wage cuts, state orders and subsidies, seizure of small savings, and autarchy – a handful of monopolists and big landowners. And in order to prolong the latter's reign (though limiting their liberty and without insuring them their pre-depression income), it has no hesitation in hastening the ruin of all other layers of the population – wage earners, consumers, savers, working farmers, artisans, and even industrialists manufacturing consumers' goods.

Those naïve people who, outside Italy and Germany, fall into the trap of fascist demagogic lies and go around saying that fascism is a "revolution," and that fascism has "gone beyond" capitalism, are advised to study the following letter from a worker published by the Nazi daily, the *Völkische Beobachter* (June 7, 1936):

"Nobody concerned with economic questions will believe the capitalist system has disappeared. Although it is true that methods of public financing have assumed a different character – a character of coercion – capital, or at least what is generally understood by this word, has never been so powerful and privileged as at the present time... The Economy accumulates enormous profits and reserves; the workers are invited to wait, and to console themselves while waiting by undergoing a whole series of preliminary conditions. The big ones make profits, and the little one receive drafts on the future. If that isn't capitalism in the specific sense of the word, I would like to know what capitalism means... One group is making formidable profits at the expense of the rest of the population. That is what used to be called capitalist exploitation..."

"This isn't National Socialism; this is simply capitalism," another correspondent wrote to the *Völkische Beobachter* on June 13. And the official organ of the Nazi party cynically replied that if the government had wanted to divide among the workers the two billions or so of big business's increased profit, it would have placed itself "in flagrant opposition to the Economy, and its energy would have been entirely paralyzed in a struggle to maintain its position."

Moreover, on the international plane, fascism merely aggravates the tendency of the whole capitalist system to national isolation and autarchy. By detaching the Economy from the international division of labour, by adapting the "productive forces to the Procrustean bed of the national state," fascism brings "chaos into world relations". For the future work of socialist planning, it creates "colossal additional difficulties".

At the same time fascism aggravates and brings to their highest degree of tension the contradictions resulting from the uneven development of the capitalist system, and thus hastens the hour of a new division of the world by force of arms – the hour of that "relapse into barbarism" which Rosa Luxemburg foresaw in case the proletariat should be slow to fulfil its class duty and achieve socialism.

Nevertheless, it is not correct to say that fascism means war. Bela Kun not long ago attacked this self-interested lie:

"The slogan that fascism, which is one of the political forms of bourgeois rule ... means war, is designed ... only to free again and always from all responsibility one of the groups of imperialist powers that mask their war preparations under democratic forms and pacifist phrases ... The old slogan of Marxist anti-militarism – that of the revolutionary struggle against imperialist war – was differently expressed: capitalism means war."

War is the product of the capitalist system as a whole. Tomorrow's war will not find the democracies opposing the dictatorships. Behind ideological pretexts, imperialist realities are concealed. Tomorrow's war will find the satisfied nations, who long ago got their "places in the sun" and divided the planet among themselves through blood and iron, opposing the "proletarian" nations – the late-comers who also demand their share in the feast, if need be through blood and iron. One group is ready to make war to force a new division of the world; the other is ready to make war to prevent this division. This is an elementary truth that can never be repeated too often in these troubled times when, for many people, anti-fascism has become synonymous with chauvinism. Fascism must be fought not from the outside by imperialist war but from within by proletarian class struggle. There is only one way to put an end to Mussolini and Hitler: that is to help the Italian and German workers to fight at home. And how can they be helped? By example! By fighting in our own countries!

Comrade Cross Invents a Problem
Felix Morrow

On February 20, 1939, the Socialist Workers Party led a demonstration of 50,000 protesting a fascist meeting at Madison Square Garden. Many liberals and Stalinist sympathizers tried to justify their refusal to participate in the antifascist demonstration by pretending that such demonstrations violated the fascists' right to free speech. This attempt to divert attention from the real issues was answered in an unsigned article probably authored by Felix Morrow: "Should Fascists be Allowed the Right of Free Speech?" Roger Cross, a member of the SWP, interpreted the position taken by the SWP as opposing the application of free speech rights to fascists. In "Comrade Cross Invents a Problem,' Morrow attempted to eliminate this misunderstanding.

I have carefully read and reread Comrade Cross' article, "The Relationship Between Free Speech and the Proletarian Revolution" [see the same number of the' Bulletin]. I regret that it is not a fruitful contribution to analyzing the new problems concretely raised by the slogan of Workers Defence Guards.[35]

That slogan does raise important new problems. Comrade Cross has, however, simply invented a nonexistent problem; he has done so, as I shall show, in order to propagate an historical interpretation of the Thermidorean reaction in Soviet Russia which is alien to the Trotskyist explanation of the degeneration of the workers state in Russia. The free' speech problem" invented by him serves merely as a springboard for a false historical theory. Comrade Cross is within his rights in raising any and all questions during the pre-convention discussion. But the main body of his article is an argument against a straw man, for it is not true that the party "denies free speech to fascists"; while the real logical motivation of his article—the enunciation of an anti-Trotskyist explanation of the degeneration of the proletarian dictatorship in Russia—is simply asserted without a word of argument or proof.

---

[35] Felix Morrow (1906 - 1988) was for many years a leading figure in US Trotskyism, best known for his book Revolution and Counter-Revolution In Spain. He joined the Communist League of America in 1933 served as editor of The Militant, the newspaper of the Socialist Workers Party (SWP). Morrow was one of 18 SWP leaders, including the party's National Secretary, James P. Cannon, imprisoned during the Second World War.

Comrade Cross writes: "The current articles in the press of the SWP have unambiguously pledged that party to most violent action in smashing the fascists and in denying them the right to speak. A more thoughtful leadership would simply agitate to smash the fascists, and leave the question of their right to speak alone. The arguments used are: that the avowed object of the fascists is to smash all democratic rights. They would deny us the right to speak, put us in concentration camps and shoot us. Consequently, why should they be allowed free speech?

Where did comrade Cross find the *Socialist Appeal* saying that fascists should not be allowed to speak? He cites no issues and pages of the Appeal —and with good reason, for he could find no such citations. Yet he blandly reports the Appeal's arguments for this nonexistent position.

A very fruitful discussion can be had on the extremely delicate problems connected with calling upon the workers to fight against the fascists: when to speak purely in defensive terms, and when to go over to terms indicating an offensive against the fascists. For the moment, it is clear, political realities—the speedy growth of the fascists, our own weakness—dictates defensive terms. A warning must also be given to the party against a too-technical conception of the formation of Workers. Defence Guards: unless the Guards are merely the first ranks, carrying with them nonparty and nonguard elements-in their actions, we shall find ourselves defeating the real purpose for mobilizing the guards: getting the masses to move with us. We must also convince the party membership—and above all the youth—that the guard is a practical, feasible, and pressing task. These and other problems, deserve discussion. But not this invention of Comrade Cross.

It has long been clearly thought out in the Bolshevik movement, where we stand on the question of free speech. First of all, "free speech" belongs to the category of "civil liberties." Let those who will, engage in this activity—we certainly don't denounce the existence of the American Civil Liberties Union —but the task of the revolutionist and of the working class and its allies is the fight for the democratic rights of the working class.

From the concept of "civil liberties," the American Civil Liberties Union logically arrives at the point offering its services to fascists who in isolated instances run afoul of a progressive mayor or police chief. What do we say about such actions of the' ACLU? We say: for every fascist persecuted by the state, ten thousand workers are persecuted. We are ready to tell the ACLU of more cases of workers rights being violated than' the ACLU can possibly handle. The ACLU knows this as well as we. But the ACLU is so anxious to prove its respectability, so fawningly worried about the good opinion of .bosses and their stooges., that the ACLU takes good money and lawyers that might be used to help persecuted workers, and diverts it to the use of the fascists.

This concrete criticism of the ACLU does not involve a denial of free speech to the fascists. Moreover, is it our business `to tell the capitalist state what to do about the fascists, to please give them free speech? Not at all. We give advice only to the workers, and we call upon to fight fascism. The only point at which we will suppress the free speech of the fascists is only in the broad sense that, in carrying out the seizure of state power, we shall undoubtedly have to smash the fascist organizations and suppress the fascist cadres.

Bonapartism, Fascism and War
Leon Trotsky

In his very pretentious, very muddled and stupid article [National Defence: The Case for Socialism, *Partisan Review*, July-August 1940] Dwight Macdonald tries to represent us as holding the view that fascism is simply a repetition of Bonapartism. A greater piece of nonsense would be hard to invent. We have analyzed fascism as it developed, throughout the various stages of its development and advanced to the forefront now one now another of its aspects. There is an element of Bonapartism in fascism. Without this element, namely, without the raising of state power above society owing to an extreme sharpening of the class struggle, fascism would have been impossible. But we pointed out from the very beginning that it was primarily a question of Bonapartism of the epoch of imperialist decline which is qualitatively different from Bonapartism of the epoch of bourgeois rise. At the next stage we separated out pure Bonapartism as the prologue to a fascist regime. Because in the case of pure Bonapartism the rule of a monarch is approximated and...[36]

in Italy ...

In post-war Italy the situation was profoundly revolutionary. The proletariat had every opportunity.

The Ministries of Bruening, Schleicher and the Presidency of Hindenburg in Germany, Petain's Government in France, but they all have proved, or must prove, unstable. In the epoch of imperialist

---

[36] First Published: Fourth International, Vol.1 No.5, October 1940, pp.128-131. Trotsky never saw this article in written form. He had dictated it into his dictaphone, as was his custom, part of it merely as notations for later elaboration. Further sections would come later, and the whole would be considerably revised, some paragraphs cut out altogether, others placed at other points in the manuscript, and so on. Trotsky did not write easily. What follows is, therefore, a literal translation of the transcription made by his Russian stenographer from the records dictated by Trotsky. Despite its unfinished form, however, this article belongs among Trotsky's most important contributions. More precisely and sharply than elsewhere, he established here the historical law that fascism is successful only after the radicalization of the masses and after the proletarian vanguard has failed to lead the radicalized masses to the conquest of power.

decline a pure Bonapartist Bonapartism is completely inadequate; imperialism finds it indispensable to mobilize the petty bourgeoisie and to crush the proletariat under its weight. Imperialism is capable of fulfilling this task only in case the proletariat itself reveals its inability to conquer power, while the social crisis drives the petty bourgeoisie into a condition of paroxysm.

The sharpness of the social crisis arises from this, that with today's concentration of the means of production, i.e., the monopoly of trusts, the law of value – the market is already incapable of regulating economic relations. State intervention becomes an absolute necessity. Inasmuch as the proletariat ...

The present war, as we have stated on more than one occasion, is a continuation of the last war. But a continuation does not signify a repetition. As a general rule, a continuation signifies a development, a deepening, a sharpening. Our policy, the policy of the revolutionary proletariat toward the second imperialist war is a continuation of the policy elaborated during the last imperialist war, primarily under Lenin's leadership. But a continuation does not signify a repetition. In this case too, continuation signifies a development, a deepening and a sharpening.

We Were Caught Unaware in 1914

During the last war not only the proletariat as a whole but also its vanguard and, in a certain sense, the vanguard of this vanguard was caught unaware. The elaboration of the principles of revolutionary policy toward the war began at a time when the war was already in full blaze and the military machine exercised unlimited rule. One year after the outbreak of the war, the small revolutionary minority was still compelled to accommodate itself to a centrist majority at the Zimmerwald Conference. Prior to the February revolution and even afterwards, the revolutionary elements felt themselves to be not contenders for power but the extreme left opposition. Even Lenin relegated the socialist revolution to a more or less distant future. (In 1915 or 1916) he wrote in Switzerland: (quotation)[37]. If that is how

---

[37] Several citations from Lenin during that period fit Trotsky's description. We quote two:
"It is possible, however, that five, ten and even more years will pass before the beginning of the socialist revolution." (From an article written in March, 1916, Lenin's Collected Works, vol.XIX, p.45, Third Russian Edition)

Lenin viewed the situation, then there is hardly any need of talking about the others.

This political position of the extreme left wing expressed itself most graphically on the question of the defence of the fatherland.

In 1915 Lenin referred in his writings to revolutionary wars which the victorious proletariat would have to wage. But it was a question of an indefinite historical perspective and not of tomorrow's task. The attention of the revolutionary wing was centered on the question of the defence of the capitalist fatherland. The revolutionists naturally replied to this question in the negative. This was entirely correct. But this purely negative answer served as the basis for propaganda and for training the cadres but it could not win the masses who did not want a foreign conqueror. In Russia prior to the war the Bolsheviks constituted four-fifths of the proletarian vanguard, that is, of the workers participating in political life (newspapers, elections, etc.). Following the February revolution the unlimited rule passed into the hands of defensists, the Mensheviks and the SR's. True enough, the Bolsheviks in the space of eight months conquered the overwhelming majority of the workers. But the decisive role in this conquest was played not by the refusal to defend the bourgeois fatherland but by the slogan: "All Power to the Soviets!" And only by this revolutionary slogan! The criticism of imperialism, its militarism, the renunciation of the defence of bourgeois democracy and so on could have never conquered the overwhelming majority of the people to the side of the Bolsheviks. In all other belligerent countries, with the exception of Russia the revolutionary wing toward the end of the war all ...

In so far as the proletariat proves incapable at a given stage of conquering power, imperialism begins regulating economic life with its own methods; the fascist party which becomes the state power is the political mechanism. The productive forces are in irreconcilable contradiction not only with private property but also with national state boundaries. Imperialism is the very expression of this contradiction. Imperialist capitalism seeks to solve this contradiction through an extension of boundaries, seizure of new territories, and so on. The totalitarian state, subjecting all aspects of economic, political and cultural life to finance capital, is the instrument for creating a super-nationalist state, an imperialist empire, the rule over continents, the rule over the whole world.

"We, the older men, will perhaps not live long enough to see the decisive battles of the impending revolution." (Report on 1905 Revolution delivered to Swiss students, January, 1917, idem, page 357)

All these traits of fascism we have analyzed each one by itself and all of them in their totality to the extent that they became manifest or came to the forefront.

The Point at Which Fascism Succeeds

Both theoretical analysis as well as the rich historical experience of the last quarter of a century have demonstrated with equal force that fascism is each time the final link of a specific political cycle composed of the following: the gravest crisis of capitalist society; the growth of the radicalization of the working class; the growth of sympathy toward the working class and a yearning for change on the part of the rural and urban petty bourgeoisie; the extreme confusion of the big bourgeoisie; its cowardly and treacherous manoeuvres aimed at avoiding the revolutionary climax; the exhaustion of the proletariat, growing confusion and indifference; the aggravation of the social crisis; the despair of the petty bourgeoisie, its yearning for change, the collective neurosis of the petty bourgeoisie, its readiness to believe in miracles; its readiness for violent measures; the growth of hostility towards the proletariat which has deceived its expectations.

These are the premises for a swift formation of a fascist party and its victory.

It is quite self-evident that the radicalization of the working class in the United States has passed only through its initial phases, almost exclusively in the sphere of the trade union movement (the CIO). The pre-war period, and then the war itself may temporarily interrupt this process of radicalization, especially if a considerable number of workers are absorbed into war industry. But this interruption of the process of radicalization cannot be of a long duration.

The second stage of radicalization will assume a more sharply expressive character. The problem of forming an independent labour party will be put on the order of the day. Our transitional demands will gain great popularity.

On the other hand, the fascist, reactionary tendencies will withdraw to the background, assuming a defensive position, awaiting a more favourable moment. This is the nearest perspective. No occupation is more completely unworthy than that of speculating whether or not we shall succeed in creating a powerful revolutionary leader party. Ahead lies a favourable perspective, providing all the justification for revolutionary activism. It is necessary to utilize the opportunities which are opening up and to build the revolutionary party.

Problem of Power Posed to the Workers

The Second World War poses the question of change of regimes more imperiously, more urgently than did the first war. It is first and foremost a question of the political regime. The workers are aware that democracy is suffering shipwreck everywhere, and that they are threatened by fascism even in those countries where fascism is as yet non-existent. The bourgeoisie of the democratic countries will naturally utilize this dread of fascism on the part of the workers, but, on the other hand, the bankruptcy of democracies, their collapse, their painless transformation into reactionary dictatorships compel the workers to pose before themselves the problem of power, render them responsive to the posing of the problem of power.

Reaction wields today such power as perhaps never before in the modern history of mankind. But it would be an inexcusable blunder to see only reaction. The historical process is a contradictory one. Under the cover of official reaction profound processes are taking place among the masses who are accumulating experience and are becoming receptive to new political perspectives. The old conservative tradition of the democratic state which was so powerful even during the era of the last imperialist war exists today only as an extremely unstable survival. On the eve of the last war the European workers had numerically powerful parties. But on the order of the day were put reforms, partial conquests, and not at all the conquest of power.

The American working class is still without a mass labour party even today. But the objective situation and the experience accumulated by the American workers can pose within a very brief period of time on the order of the day the question of the conquest of power. This perspective must be made the basis of our agitation. It is not merely a question of a position on capitalist militarism and of renouncing the defence of the bourgeois state but of directly preparing for the conquest of power and the defence of the proletarian fatherland.

May not the Stalinists turn out at the head of a new revolutionary upsurge and may they not ruin the revolution as they did in Spain and previously in China? It is of course impermissible to consider that such a possibility is excluded, for example in France. The first wave of the revolution has often, or more correctly, always carried to the top those "left" parties which have not managed to discredit themselves completely in the preceding period and which have an imposing political tradition behind them. Thus the February revolution raised up the Mensheviks, the S. R.'s who were the opponents of the revolution on its very eve. Thus the German revolution in November,

1918, raised to power the social democrats who were the irreconcilable opponents of revolutionary uprisings.

Twelve years ago Trotsky wrote in an article published by The New Republic:

"There is no epoch in human history so saturated with antagonisms as ours. Under a too high tension of class and international animosities, the 'fuses' of democracy 'blow out'. Hence the short-circuits of dictatorship. Naturally the weakest 'interrupters' are the first to give way. But the force of internal and world controversies does not weaken: it grows. It is doubtful if it is destined to calm down, given that the process has so far only taken hold of the periphery of the capitalist world. Gout begins in the little finger of a hand or in the big toe, but once on the way it goes right to the heart." (*The New Republic*, May 22, 1929)

The American Philistine Protests

This was written at a time when the entire bourgeois democracy in each country believed that fascism was possible only in the backward countries which had not yet graduated from the school of democracy. The editorial board of The New Republic, which at that period had not yet been touched with the blessings of the GPU, accompanied Trotsky's article with one of its own. The article is so characteristic of the average American philistine that we shall quote from it the most interesting passages.

"In view of his personal misfortunes, the exiled Russian leader shows a remarkable power of detached analysis; but his detachment is that of the rigid Marxian, and seems to us to lack a realistic view of history-the very thing on which he prides himself. His notion that democracy is a fair-weather form of government, incapable of withstanding the storms of international or domestic controversy, can be supported (as he himself half admits) only by taking for your examples countries where democracy has never made more than the feeblest beginnings, and countries, moreover, in which the industrial revolution has hardly more than started."

Further on, the editorial board of *The New Republic* dismisses the instance of Kerensky's democracy in Soviet Russia and why it failed to withstand the test of class contradictions arid yielded place to a revolutionary perspective. The periodical sagely writes:

"Kerensky's weakness was an historic accident, which Trotsky cannot admit because there is no room in his mechanistic scheme for any such thing."

Just like Dwight Macdonald, *The New Republic* accused the Marxists of being unable to understand history realistically owing to their orthodox or mechanistic approach to political events. The New Republic was of the opinion that fascism is the product of the backwardness of capitalism and not its over-ripeness. In the opinion of that periodical which, I repeat, was the opinion of the overwhelming majority of average democratic philistines, fascism is the lot of backward bourgeois countries. The sage editorial board did not even take the trouble of thinking about the question of why it was the universal conviction in the Nineteenth Century that backward countries must develop along the road of democracy. In any case, in the old capitalist countries democracy came into its sights at a time when the level of their economic development was not above but below the economic development of modern Italy. And what is more, in that era democracy represented the main highway of historical development which was entered by all countries one by one, the backward ones following the more advanced, and sometimes ahead of them. Our era on the contrary, is the era of democracy's collapse, and moreover, the collapse begins with the weaker links but gradually extends to those which appeared strong and impregnable. Thus the orthodox or mechanistic, that is, the Marxist approach to events enabled us to forecast the course of developments many years in advance. On the contrary, the realistic approach of *The New Republic* represented the approach of a blind kitten. The New Republic followed up its critical attitude toward Marxism by falling under the influence of the most revolting caricature of Marxism, namely, Stalinism.

The Newest Crop of Philistines

Most of the philistines of the newest crop base their attacks on Marxism on the fact that contrary to Marx's prognosis fascism came instead of socialism. Nothing is more stupid and vulgar than this criticism. Marx demonstrated and proved that when capitalism reaches a certain level the only way out for society lies in the socialization of the means of production, i.e., socialism. He also demonstrated that in view of the class structure of society the proletariat alone is capable of solving this task in an irreconcilable revolutionary struggle against the bourgeoisie. He further demonstrated that for the fulfilment of this task the proletariat needs a revolutionary party.

All his life Marx, and together with him and after him Engels, and after them Lenin, waged an irreconcilable struggle against those traits in proletarian parties, socialist parties which obstructed the solution of the revolutionary historical task. The irreconcilability of the struggle waged by Marx, Engels, and Lenin against opportunism, on the one side, and anarchism, on the other, demonstrates that they did not at all underestimate this danger. In what did it consist? In this, that the opportunism of the summits of the working class, subject to the bourgeoisie's influence, could obstruct, slow down, make more difficult, postpone the fulfilment of the revolutionary task of the proletariat. It is precisely this condition of society that we are now observing.

Fascism did not at all come "instead" of socialism. Fascism is the continuation of capitalism, an attempt to perpetuate its existence by means of the most bestial and monstrous measures.

Capitalism obtained an opportunity to resort to fascism only because the proletariat did not accomplish the socialist revolution in time. The proletariat was paralyzed in the fulfilment of its task by the opportunist parties. The only thing that can be said is that there turned out to be more obstacles, more difficulties, more stages on the road of the revolutionary development of the proletariat than was foreseen by the founders of scientific socialism.

Fascism and the series of imperialist wars constitute the terrible school in which the proletariat has to free itself of petty bourgeois traditions and superstitions, has to rid itself of opportunist, democratic and adventurist parties, has to hammer out and train the revolutionary vanguard and in this way prepare for the solving of the task apart from which there is not, and cannot be, any salvation for the development of mankind.

Eastman, if you please, has come to the conclusion that the concentration of the means of production in the hands of the state endangers his "freedom" and he has therefore decided to renounce socialism. This anecdote deserves being included in the text of a history of ideology. The socialization of the means of production is the only solution to the economic problem at the given stage of mankind's development. The delay in solving this problem leads to the barbarism of fascism. All the intermediate solutions undertaken by the bourgeoisie with the help of the petty bourgeoisie have suffered a miserable and shameful fiasco. All this is absolutely uninteresting to Eastman. He noticed that his "freedom" (freedom of muddling, freedom of indifferentism, freedom of passivity, freedom of literary dilettantism) was being threatened from various sides, and he decided immediately to apply his own measure: renounce socialism. Astonishingly enough this decision exercised no influence either on Wall Street or on the policy of the trade unions. Life went its own way just as if Max Eastman had remained a socialist. It may be set down as a general rule that the more impotent is a petty bourgeois radical especially in the United States the more.

Fascism Has Not Conquered in France

In France there is no fascism in the real sense of the term. The regime of the senile Marshal Petain represents a senile form of Bonapartism of the epoch of imperialist decline. But this regime too proved possible only after the prolonged radicalization of the French working class, which led to the explosion of June 1936, had failed to find a revolutionary way out. The Second and Third Internationals, the reactionary charlatanism of the "People's Fronts" deceived and demoralized the working class. After five years of propaganda in favor of an alliance of democracies and of collective security, after Stalin's sudden passage into Hitler's camp, the French working class proved caught unaware. The war provoked a terrible disorientation and the mood of passive defeatism, or to put it more correctly, the indifferentism of an impasse. From this web of circumstances arose first the unprecedented military catastrophe and then the despicable Petain regime.

Precisely because Petain's regime is senile Bonapartism, it contains no element of stability and can be overthrown by a revolutionary mass uprising much sooner than a fascist regime.

Especially Important to US Workers

In every discussion of political topics the question invariably flares up: Shall we succeed in creating a strong party for the moment when the crisis comes? Might not fascism anticipate us? Isn't a fascist stage of development inevitable? The successes of fascism easily make people lose all perspective, lead them to forget the actual conditions which made the strengthening and the victory of fascism possible. Yet a clear understanding of these conditions is of special importance to the workers of the United States. We may set it down as an historical law: Fascism was able to conquer only in those countries where the conservative labour parties prevented the proletariat from utilizing the revolutionary situation and seizing power. In Germany two revolutionary situations were involved: 1918-1919 and 1923-24. Even in 1929 a direct struggle for power on the part of the proletariat was still possible. In all these three cases the social democracy and the Comintern criminally and viciously disrupted the conquest of power and thereby placed society in an impasse. Only under these conditions and in this situation did the stormy rise of Fascism and its gaining of power prove possible.

Fascism and Socialism
Daniel Guérin

Fascism and Big Business was begun in 1934 after February 6, and appeared in July 1936. Was it necessary to reprint the book in its present form or continue the investigation to the start of 1945?[38]

The date on which we stopped writing was undoubtedly premature. The phenomenon of fascism was then still in the full course of development (above all in Germany). Certain of its traits had not yet been sufficiently revealed. It was necessary to probe further.

But perhaps there was an impediment in probing too extensively. The object of this book, if we can so express it, is the study of fascism in its pure form. Our purpose was not to write the contemporary history of Italy and Germany; but to better understand, with the aid of parallel observations of these two countries, the essential nature of fascism.[39]

For, after 1939, the phenomenon of fascism tends to become confounded with the great upheaval of the imperialist. war. Nothing so resembles a country at war as another country at war. The characteristic traits of fascism are, in large part (not completely) blurred by those now familiar traits, namely, universally unloosed militarism and war economy. Undoubtedly a materialist explanation of the war should be undertaken as well as the materialist explanation of fascism. But whoever embraces too much grasps too little. We leave this task to others.[40] We have consciously limited the scope of this work to the study of the phenomenon of fascism by itself.

An objection might perhaps be raised that fascism and war are inseparable, that the present war is the monstrous product of fascism. But that's precisely what we deny. There is, certainly, a direct link

---

[38] From Fourth International, Vol.6 No.9, September 1945, pp.269-273.

[39] It has been objected that this book is somewhat schematic. We are not certain that this criticism is well founded. It would be if we had proposed to press into the same mould the evolution of the two countries studied, without taking into account their dissimilarities in every domain. Such was not our purpose. In confining ourselves to their common traits which are specifically the traits of the phenomenon of fascism, we never intended to depict Italian Fascism and German National Socialism as strictly identical. We have proceeded no differently than physicians who, on the basis of specific observations, noted in respect to dissimilar patients, establish the same general symptoms of a given disease.

[40] Cf. Henri Claude: *From The Economic Crisis To The World War*, 1929-1939, an attempt at a materialist explanation of modern war.

between war and fascism. They grow out of the same dungheap; they are, each in its own way, the monstrous products of the capitalist system in decline. They both flow from the fundamental vice of the system: first, the incompatibility between the tremendous development of the productive forces, and private ownership of the means of production: second, the partitioning of the world into national states. They both aspire, by different roads, to break the iron ring of the contradictions in which this system is henceforth enclosed. They both aim to restore endangered capitalist profits. Finally, both of these phenomena, while aiming to prolong the system, actually hasten the heur of its collapse. Moreover, beyond these general ties, a more direct interconnection can be observed between fascism and war in Italy and in Germany: because these two countries lack raw materials and markets, because they are in the category of "hungry nations" as opposed to the "sated" nations, the crisis in which the whole capitalist system is convulsed takes on in their case a particularly acute character, and imposes upon them, in advance of the others, a "strong state." They act as "aggressive" powers with the aim of seizing part of the plunder from the "sated" nations. They aim at a new division of the world by force of arms, while their adversaries, opposing this redivision, assume the attitude of "peace-loving" powers.

Fascism and War

Thus fascism and war are, to be sure, related. But the relationship is not one of cause and effect. Eliminate fascism (assuming that could be done) and the causes of rivalries and of imperialist wars will not in the least thereby be eliminated. For four years, from 1914 to 1918, two groups of great powers fought over possession of the world market. In neither camp was there a "fascist" country. In reality, fascism and war are both the effects, different effects, of the same cause: though the two phenomena criss-cross, though, at times, they seem to be confounded with each other (and every conscious effort is made to confuse them) still each has a distinct existence and demands a separate study.

The study of the phenomenon of fascism should be continued beyond 1936. But, aside from a few additional facts, some confirmations and dotting of the i's, we have not believed it necessary – for the reason indicated above – to bring the investigation up to date. That is why we have adopted a compromise: we have taken as a basis for the present reprint, the text of the American translation which appeared at the beginning of 1939 under the title of *Fascism and Big Business*. This translation was made with the aid of documentation up to the end of 1938. The original text was then very carefully revised (above all in that which concerns Germany). We confine ourselves merely to adding to it several corrections which seem indispensable at the beginning of 1945.

Do the events since 1939 cast a new light on the phenomenon of fascism? At the risk of disappointing the reader, we reply in the negative. At the risk of appearing presumptuous or of clinging to outlived positions, we will say that the events of these last years, in our opinion, do not modify to any marked degree the conclusions of our book. The only thing that fascism has brought, since 1939, is renewed proof of its barbarism. But who can be surprised at this, after witnessing the manner in which it crushed the Italian and German proletariat before crushing Europe? And can this barbarism which is "fascist" in its most hideous traits, be considered solely "fascist"? The whole war is barbarous.

Apart from that, the war and the German occupation, by giving us the opportunity to observe the phenomenon more closely, taught us, as we had already suspected, that the fascist regime, despite its "totalitarian" pretensions is not homogeneous. It never succeeded in dissolving into one single alloy the different elements of which it was composed. Its different wheels did not function without friction. Despite Hitler's attempts for several years to find a compromise formula between the party and the army, the Wehrmacht on the one hand, and the Gestapo and the SS on the other, continued their cat and dog fight. Behind this conflict is a class question. The fascist regime, despite appearances, appearances that it delighted in maintaining, never domesticated the bourgeoisie. When we upheld the thesis several years ago, that fascism is an instrument of big business, it was objected that in Italy as in Germany (in Germany above all) big business marches in step. This is not exactly true. The bourgeoisie remained an autonomous force, pursuing its own ends in the totalitarian state. It made others don the brown shirt, for the Hitler bands were indispensable to crush the proletariat, but thus far it has not donned the brown shirt itself (or, if it has, it was only for the gallery). Hermann Rauschning led us into error with his thesis according to which the ruling class was eliminated by the Nazi plebeians, people who respected nothing, "nihilists." Undoubtedly there have been individual cases where big capitalists have been ill-treated or forced to emigrate. But big business, taken as a whole, was not engulfed by the brown tide. Quite the contrary.

Army and the Regime

At all times the army is the instrument par excellence of the ruling class. The relative independence of the army with regard to the regime, its refusal to permit itself to be thoroughly nazified, makes clear the autonomy of big business (and the big landlords) towards the fascist regime, its refusal to be brought into line. We will be told: Hitler dealt some secret blows within his General Staff; insubordinate generals were successively eliminated. No doubt; but this continual "purge" was only a confirmation of the resistance that the army, backed by the big bourgeoisie, put up against complete nazification.

But what about July 20, what about those generals, those big capitalists, those country squires who were hung or shot, following the attempted assassination of Hitler? July 20, 1944, in Germany, just like July 25, 1943, in Italy (the day that Marshall Badoglio and the King had Mussolini arrested) carries striking proof that the capitalist ruling class was never absorbed by the self-styled totalitarian state. After subsidizing fascism and pushing it into power, the bourgeoisie tolerated, in spite of minor inconveniences, the overrunning of the state by the Nazi plebs: this conformed to its interests. But from the day when it appeared that the inconveniences of the regime outweighed the advantages the bourgeoisie, with the support of the army, did not hesitate to throw it overboard. As early as 1936, in the conclusions of our book, we set forth this hypothesis. The move succeeded in Italy. It has failed, for the time being, in Germany. But since the attempted assassination of July 20, Hitler is virtually finished. Big business, the top circles of the army, do not follow him any longer.[41] He only survives artificially by means of unheard of terror that the police and Himmler's SS exercise within the very midst of the army and the population as a whole. He survives only because the plans for the dismemberment of Germany, agitated from abroad, have aroused in the masses, a desperate reflex of the instinct of self-preservation. The regime, although abandoned by the people, has been able to take momentary advantage of this. He survives only because the ruling class fears to let loose open civil war in the midst of total foreign war. This last episode proves that the redoubtable instrument of repression forged by fascism can prolong the life of the latter for a moment, even after it has been abandoned by big business. The bullet destined for the workers can also serve to make a hole in the skin of a few capitalists. But not for long. No political regime can govern against the class which holds the economic power. Although it may not please some naive people, the old laws which have always governed the relations of classes, have not failed this time either. Fascism has not

---

[41] "Since the attempted assassination, Hitler knows that ... the nobility and the military caste, the big industrialists, the bankers ... are against him." Extract from an account of the July 20 attempt, by Mr. Lochner, Associated Press war correspondent, published in *Le Monde*, Mach 21, 1945.

suspended them, as with a wave of the magic wand. The link between fascism and big business is so intimate that the day when big business withdraws its support is the beginning of the end for fascism.

Fundamental Thesis

From our fundamental thesis, according to which fascism is essentially the instrument of heavy industry, certain people wish to infer today that it would suffice, in Germany, to confiscate heavy industry to extirpate every germ of fascism. We strongly protest against this false and tendentious deduction. Undoubtedly, heavy industry is the most aggressive, the most reactionary segment of capitalism. It incontestably subsidized and then hoisted to power the fascist bands. But the "confiscation" of its wealth would not suffice (quite the contrary) to resolve the contradictions in which the whole of German capitalism is struggling. Furthermore, who will profit from this confiscation? "The majority of shares, it is said, would inevitably fall into the hands of the Allies." This is the clue. What's involved here is not a matter of political cleansing aimed at destroying the germs of fascism, but an attempt of the Anglo-American powers to strangle their German competitor. Not long ago, for similar motives, the industrial region of the Ruhr was occupied by the troops of Poincairé. This action, as is well-known, served as a springboard for National Socialism. Only the proletarian revolution can free the world once and for all from the Hitlerite nightmare.

We pointed out, in the conclusion of this book, fascism's extraordinary will to endure. The desperate tenacity with which it defends itself today, although knowing itself lost, evidently surpasses all expectations. Nevertheless the phenomenon is comprehensible if one remembers that fascism is not only an instrument at the service of big business, but, at the same time a mystical upheaval of the pauperized and discontented petty-bourgeoisie. Although a large part of the middle class who had helped fascism to power is cruelly deceived today, such is not the case with the militant sector. There are many playboys and corrupt people in the enormous bureaucratic apparatus of the Fascist state, but there are also some real fanatics. These not only defend their social position, even their lives, in defending the regime, they also defend an idea to which they firmly cling to the death. (Let us note in passing: it is not by brute force, much less foreign bayonets, that one loses faith. Only the powerful wind of the proletarian revolution in Germany would be able to clear their brains.)

Fascism, in the countries where it attained power, stands a chance of surviving for another reason: in its decline, as at its birth, it owes much to the complacence of its "adversaries": the "democratic" state which succeeded it remains completely infected with the fascist virus (just as the "democratic" state which had preceded it was entirely infected with the fascist virus). The "purge" is nothing but a shameful comedy, because to really disinfect the bourgeois state, it is necessary to destroy it. The administrative tops, the army, the police, the judiciary remains staffed with auxiliaries and accomplices of the former regime, the same personnel for the most part who, a short time ago, delivered the keys of power to fascism. In Italy, Marshall Badoglio is the man who once placed the cadres and resources of the army at the disposition of the "black shirts." Who can be surprised if, as Mussolini's successor, he lets the Duce escape from prison? Bonomi, in 1921-1922, knowingly paved the way for fascism. Who can be surprised if in 1945, under his government, with the complicity of his functionaries, the fascist general Roatta succeeded in escaping? When will the complacent Bruening return to Germany? Only the revolutionary proletariat will be able to nail to the wall the fascist bandits and their accomplices without any delays or hesitation.[42]

Fascism's New Forms

After its downfall as the political regime, fascism appears to borrow entirely new forms. It seems to have learned much from the tactics adopted by the Resistance movement in the occupied countries. It studies the lessons of the Maquis. Already, the fascists in Germany are organizing themselves for future underground struggle. It is possible that we shall see something of this kind even in France. Perhaps we are not as fully rid of the bands of Doriot and Darnand as we thought. Can such undertakings be successful? The problem is not technical, it is political. The Maquis owed their success above all to the fact that they were supported by a part of the population. Insurgent fascism could not stand up against a powerful movement of anti-fascist and revolutionary masses. But if such a mass movement does not develop or if other factors (of which we will speak a little further on) push a part of the middle classes and peasantry back towards reaction, then underground fascism could become a real danger.

Perhaps in the conclusions of this book, there is a point which has not been sufficiently stressed: the underground development of the class struggle beneath the fascist lid. We stressed, and it was necessary to stress, the formidable methods employed by the totalitarian

---

[42] The execution of Mussolini by the red partisans, an event which occurred after this preface was already written, confirms our thesis. As was to be expected, this resort to direct action displeased "the right kind" of people.

regimes to break up, to "atomize" the movement of the working class, to scientifically track it down, if one can so express it, and to destroy in the embryo every form of opposition. But gradually and to the extent that the fascist lid is lifted, we perceive that beneath it, the class struggle, supposedly destroyed forever, continues right on its way. As we are writing these lines, Northern Italy has not yet been liberated. But we have already heard many echoes of the extraordinary fighting power displayed in these last years by the workers of Milan, of Turin, within the great industrial combines on which the red flag waved in 1920. More than twenty years of fascist dictatorship have not succeeded in changing the Italian worker.

In Germany, the grip of the regime and the police terror have been infinitely stronger. But, in spite of the savage muzzling of the German people[43], we find once more traces of a revolutionary vanguard, especially in the concentration camps and the prisons. Fascism has not halted humanity's continuous march toward emancipation. It has only delayed it temporarily, if at all.

Is it necessary to reissue this book at the moment when the fate of Mussolini and Hitler would appear to discourage their imitators in other countries? Outside of its retrospective interest, does it retain its timeliness?

Re-reading it, we are impressed with the fact that its real subject is socialism much more than it is fascism. For what is fascism, at bottom, but the direct product of the failure to achieve socialism? Behind fascism, the shadow of socialism is ceaselessly present. We have only studied the first in relation to the second. More than once, in the course of these pages, fascism has served us simply as a counterpoint with which to define better by contrast certain essential aspects of socialism. When, as we hope, the day comes in which nothing remains of fascism but a bad memory, this book will remain an attempt to contrast socialism to what was, at one time, its most redoubtable opponent. On this score perhaps *Fascism and Big Business* will not become outdated too quickly.

---

[43] Not only the repression of the Gestapo, but also the mobilization of all able-bodied men, the dispersion in the country of the population of the destroyed urban and industrial centers, the systematic efforts of the Allies to prevent the revolution in Germany even at the price of dragging out the monstrous slaughter, the bludgeoning effects of the defeat, the desperate flight before the Red Army, which spoke in terms of vengeance and not of liberation, all these factors have contributed to demoralize and to momentarily paralyze the German proletariat. But perhaps certain people rejoice too soon at its present apathy. – (End of May, 1945.)

A Widespread Illusion

But, as a matter of fact, is it really certain that the fascist epidemic has been definitively checked? We can only hope so, but we cannot at all be certain of it. It is a widespread illusion that the defeat of "The Axis" sounds the death knell of fascism in the entire world. Fascism, if you will pardon us for repeating it, is not a product that is specifically Italian or specifically German. It is the specific product only of decaying capitalism, of the crisis of the capitalist system which has become a permanent one. It has a double origin in the determination of big business to revive the profit mechanism by exceptional measures and in the revolt of the pauperized and despairing middle classes. In the aftermath of this second world war, capitalism in Europe will be convulsed with far greater contradictions which will differ in their acuteness from those that followed the last world war. It will need a "strong state" to survive. "Controlled economy," this rickety expedient which it can no longer dispense with, is incompatible with "democratic" politics. It requires a stable central power which is not subject to the control of the masses. "Controlled economy" is not specifically fascist; it exists, in varying degrees, in all countries. But it accommodates itself much better to fascist regimes than to "democratic" regimes.

On the other hand, the tremendous impoverishment of large sections of the middle classes (much more advanced than that observed in Italy and in Germany in the period "between the two wars") will create a state of profound social instability. Big business could very well, once again, bring to its feet the petty bourgeoisie driven to frenzy, arm them, inspire them with fanaticism, if, unfortunately, the worker's parties prove incapable, once again, of showing them another way out.

Let us turn our attention also to the youth. Our young rebels have gotten into the habit of living outside the law; they have been shaped by the grim and extraordinary experiences of the Maquis. Today, they experience some difficulty and distaste in readapting themselves to prosaic "normal life." The inglorious conclusion of the Resistance struggle plunges them, moreover, into discouragement and doubt. Let us not forget that, following the armistice of 1918, the volunteer corps of world war veterans, for similar psychological reasons, provided Mussolini and Hitler with their first recruits. Beware!

Foreign Aid

Fascism, moreover, can secure support abroad. The big "democracies" do not always tell the truth. They fought Hitler, not, as they claim today, because of the authoritarian and brutal form of the National Socialist regime, but because German imperialism, at a given moment, dared to dispute with them the hegemony of the world. It has been too generally forgotten that Hitler was hoisted to power with the blessings of the international bourgeoisie. During the first years of his rule, Anglo-American capitalism from the British aristocracy to Henry Ford, gave him, according to all evidence, their support. They viewed him as "the strong man," who alone was capable of reestablishing order in Europe and saving the continent from Bolshevism.[44] Only much later, when the capitalists of the "democratic" countries found their interests, their markets, their sources of raw materials menaced by the irresistible expansion of German imperialism, did they start to preach against National Socialism, to denounce it as "immoral" and "un-Christian." And, even then, there were capitalists and princes of the Church, who, more anxious to ward off the "red peril" than the German peril, remained partial towards the policeman of Europe.

Today the big "democracies" proclaim themselves "antifascist." That's the word they're always mouthing. In reality, anti-fascism became necessary as a platform for them to overcome their German competitor. They could not gain the full allegiance of the popular masses in the struggle against Hitlerism solely by exalting national sentiment. Despite all appearances, we are no longer in the age of national wars. The struggle of the classes, the social war, dominates our epoch. The toiling masses could not have been brought to sacrifice themselves to liberate Europe unless sentiments of a social order were aroused in them, unless an appeal was made to their class instinct. They were told that it was necessary to finish off fascism. And as they understood more or less clearly, that Fascism is the exacerbated form of detested capitalism, they consented to all sacrifices. The Parisian barricades of the end of August 1944, the exploits of the various Maquis, will live as admirable examples of proletarian devotion.

But tomorrow the big "democracies" may very well put anti-fascism back on the shelf. Already, this magic word, which inspired the workers to rise up against Hitlerism, is considered by them undesirable as soon as it becomes the rallying point of the adversaries of the capitalist system. Already in Belgium and Greece, the Allies did not hesitate to brutally crush the very resistance movement which they had been only too happy to utilize for their own purposes. To reestablish "order," they will sooner or later be compelled (as is already the case in Greece) to find points of support in the midst of the

---

[44] It is also forgotten that the "upper crust" of Paris, London and New York paraded before the Palazza Venetia to cast admiring looks at the Caesar who had made the trains run on time.

liberated populations. Against the people's vanguard they will support formations of a clearly fascist character. Naturally they will be baptised with another name, for the word fascist is definitively "played out." But, under the new label, the old merchandise will remain the same. It is to be expected that, tomorrow, the Allies will see in a neo-fascism more or less camouflaged, a guarantee against the "chaos" and "anarchy" rising in Europe; that is to say, against the proletarian revolution.

Big business, native as well as Anglo-American, will of course hesitate, in one country or another, to hand over the power to fascism (the distasteful experiences of Italy and Germany will undoubtedly make them somewhat cautious on this score) but it is quite likely that it will at least utilize the fascist gangs as anti-labor militias. In short, fascism, by whatever name it is called, will remain the reserve army of decaying capitalism.

The Basic Conclusion

Thus our basic conclusion is seen to be confirmed by the most recent developments, namely, that fascism, outgrowth of the failure to achieve socialism, can be effectively fought and vanquished definitively only by the proletarian revolution.

The evil cannot be warded off by palliatives and patch-work. The world tosses about in chaos and the intervention of the "strong state" is made necessary because the capitalist abscess has immeasurably prolonged itself. The abscess can not be removed except by the surgical intervention of the proletariat. Outside of this radical solution there is no salvation; all "anti-fascism" that rejects it is but vain and deceitful babbling. The misfortune is that we have permitted the bourgeois-democrats to seize hold of anti-fascism. These gentlemen fear the fascist knout for their own skins, but they fear the proletarian revolution at least as much. They conjured up a bastard solution to reconcile these two fears, that of the "Popular Fronts." The "Popular Fronts" declaim against fascism but without taking a single thoroughgoing measure to attack its material roots. They refrain from laying a hand on capitalism despite their demagogic tirades against the "two hundred families," against the "trusts," and, an even graver crime, by their economic and social policies, they deepen the causes of friction between the proletariat and the middle classes; and thus they push the latter towards the very fascism from which they pretend to divert them.

The fascist menace has made many people discover the problem of the middle classes. Only recently, the parties of the left saw in them only an easy, faithful and stable electoral clientele. But from the day when it was demonstrated that in the course of their oscillations, amplified by the economic crisis, the middle classes could enter the opposite camp, that they could be seized with collective madness, that they could don the fascist uniform, these same parties have known the anguish of the mother hen menaced with losing her chicks; the question has become an obsession with them – how to retain the middle classes? Unfortunately, they have understood nothing (nor do they wish to understand anything) of the problem. We must apologize for only having, in this book, skimmed the surface of this problem. In effect, the logic of our analysis has led us less to research concerning how socialism could have been able to turn the middle classes away from fascism than to showing why and how it, fascism, succeeded in conquering them. The reader will therefore permit us a brief digression here.

The middle classes and the proletariat have common interests against big business. But there is more involved than common interests. They are not "anti-capitalist" in the same fashion. Undoubtedly the bourgeoisie exploits, sharpens at will these differences of interests, but it does not create them out of the whole cloth. It is therefore impossible to bring together the proletariat and the petty bourgeoisie around a common program which will completely satisfy both. One of the two parties must make concessions. The proletariat, naturally, can agree to some. Whenever possible, it must see that the blows it directs against big business do not strike at the same time the small investors, artisans, merchants, peasants. But on certain essential points, it must remain intransigent, for if it yields on these points in order to retain influence over the middle classes, to reassure the small shopkeepers or peasants, it would renounce dealing capitalism the decisive blows. And every time that it failed in its mission to destroy capitalism, every time it has not pushed its advantage right to the end, the middle classes, caught between menacing big business and an aggressive working class, have become enraged and turned toward fascism.

Revolutionary Action

In short, the proletariat cannot win over the middle classes by renouncing its own socialist program. The proletariat must convince the middle classes of its capacity to lead society onto a new road; by the strength and firmness of its revolutionary action. But it is precisely this that the inventors of the "Popular Fronts" do not wish to understand. They have but one idea in their heads: to catch the middle classes on bait-hooks, and they do this with so much skill that they eventually throw them back towards the fascist bait.

When they face the dilemma, fascism or socialism, these rabbit-skinned democrats get red with anger. What right has anyone to disturb the pure waters of their "anti-fascism"? But the day comes when (such was the sad fate of some among them) they themselves succumb to the fascist knout. Let us honor their memory while denouncing their bankruptcy.

Anti-fascism cannot triumph as long as it drags along as the tail to the kite of bourgeois democracy. Beware of "anti" formulas. They are always inadequate because they are purely negative. One cannot conquer a principle except by opposing to it another principle – a superior principle. The world of today, in the midst of its convulsions, is not only looking for a form of property that corresponds to the collective character and the gigantic scale of modern production; it seeks also a form of government capable of substituting a rational order for chaos, while liberating man. Bourgeois parliamentarianism offers only a caricature of democracy, ever more impotent and more corrupt. Deceived and disheartened, the world turns towards the strong State, the heaven-sent man, towards the "leader principle." On the plane of ideas, Fascism will be defeated only on that day when we present to humanity and when by example we shall make triumphant a new form of government of men, an authentic democracy, complete, direct, in which all the producers take part in the administration of things. This new type of democracy is not a chimera, an invention of the spirit. It exists. The great French Revolution – as we will demonstrate in another work – let us hear its first birth cries. The Commune of 1871 was the first attempt at its application, as Marx and Lenin have shown in a masterly manner. The Russian Soviets of 1917 provided the model to the world in unforgettable fashion. Since then, Soviet democracy has gone through a prolonged eclipse in Russia itself, for reasons too numerous to outline here. This eclipse coincides with the rise of Fascism.

Today fascism lies crippled. We will give it the finishing blow by proving in action that true democracy, democracy of the Commune or soviet type, is viable and superior to all other types of government of men. All Power to the Soviets, said Lenin. Mussolini shamefully caricatured this slogan, making of it the slogan of the totalitarian state: all power to fascism.

The totalitarian state is a tottering monster. We shall be forever rid of it by assuring the triumph of the antithesis: the Republic of the Workers' Councils.

The Menace of Fascism
Ted Grant

Mosley's Early Supporters

Only two years after the war allegedly fought to destroy fascism, the British fascists have commenced to regroup their forces. Throughout the country, cautiously and unobtrusively at first, but more and more boldly, the fascists have come into the open.[45]

At first they emerged as local and separate organisations and adopted a host of names for reasons of expediency. The aim was clearly to prepare for unification at a later stage. Among the most important of these organisations were the British League of Ex-Servicemen and women; Mosley's Book Club and Discussion Group; the Union of British Freedom; the Sons of St George (Derby); the Imperial Defence League (Manchester); the British Workers' Party of National Unity (Bristol); the Corporate Club (a student group at Oxford University).

These organisations are not short of money. Before the war the British Union of Fascists (BUF) had extensive funds at its disposal. The fascists had intimate links with big business. Mosley boasted that he had spent £96,000 of his own personal fortune "in support of my beliefs during my political life". On two occasions Mosley himself married into millionaire families. In 1920 he married Lady Cynthia Curzon, a daughter of the late Marquis Curzon of Kedleston and a granddaughter of Levi Zeigler Leiter, a Jewish Chicago millionaire. Lady Cynthia inherited £28,000 a year from her own family (there are two children of this marriage). After the death of his first wife a few years prior to the war, Mosley married again, this time, into the Guinness millions. His wife is the sister of the notorious Unity Mitford, friend of Hitler.

In the early days of the fascist movement, Mosley was enthusiastically backed by a number of prominent capitalist and military figures. True, later when Mosley became discredited and it was clear that the movement was not timely, many of them dropped away or fell into the background. Apart from the open members of the Fascist Party, a powerful club composed of members of the ruling class

---

[45] Source: Revolutionary Communist Party pamphlet, June 1948. Ted Grant (1913–2006) was a South African Trotskyist who played a leading role in the British section of the Fourth International from the 1940s until the mid1960s. He founded Militant, a marxist newspaper in the Labour party, in 1964.

was formed to back the blackshirts. In a pamphlet entitled Who Backs Mosley published by Labour Research, some enlightening facts were revealed:

"On New Year's day 1934 was formed the January Club, whose object is to form a solid blackshirt front. The chairman Sir John Squire, editor of the London Mercury said that it was not a fascist organisation but admitted that 'the members who belonged to all political parties were for the most part in sympathy with the fascist movement'. (The Times, 22 March, 1934) The January Club held its dinners at the Savoy and the Hotel Splendide. The Tatler shows pictures of the club assemblies, distinguished by evening dress, wines, flowers and a general air of luxury. The leader is enjoying himself among his own class..."

The members of this club were:

COLONEL LORD MIDDLETON, a director of the Yorkshire Insurance Co, Malton Investment Trust, British Coal Refining Processes Ltd, and three other companies. He owns about 15,000 acres of land and minerals in Nottinghamshire.

GENERAL SIR HUBERT DE LA POER GOUGH, GCMG, KCB, KCVO, Commander of the Fifth Army 1916-18 and Chief of the Allied Mission to the Baltic, 1919 (Russian intervention), now director of Siemens Bros, Caxton Electric Development Ltd, Enfield Rolling Mills, and two other companies.

AIR COMMODORE CHAMIER, CB, CMG, OBE, DSO, late Indian Army. Now aviation consultant and agent to, and lately director of, Vickers Aviation Ltd.

VINCENT C VICKERS, director of the London Assurance Corporation and a large shareholder in Vickers Ltd.

LORD LLOYD, former Governor of Bombay...

THE EARL OF GLASGOW, Privy Councillor, brother-in-law to Sir Thomas Inskip, the Attorney General, who was responsible for the Sedition Bill in the House of Commons. The Earl owns Kelburn Castle, Ayrshire, and about 2500 acres.

MAJOR NATHAN, Liberal MP for NE Bethnal Green...a member of the Jewish Agency under the mandate for Palestine...Chairman of the Anglo-Chinese Finance and Trade Corporation...

WARD PRICE, special correspondent to the Daily Mail and director of Associated Newspapers and British Movietone News.

WING COMMANDER SIR LOUIS GRIEG, KBE, CBO, RAF, partner in J and H Scrimageour, stockbrokers, director of Handley Page Ltd, and an insurance company and Gentleman Usher in Ordinary to the King.

LADY RAVENDALE, Baroness, sister-in-law to Mosley and granddaughter to Levi Leiter.

COUNT and COUNTESS PAUL MUNSTER.

MAJOR METCALFE, MVO, MC, brother-in-law of Lady Cynthia Mosley and Lady Ravendale, late aide-de-camp to the Prince of Wales and the Commander in Chief in India.

SIR PHILIP MAGNUS, Bart, a leading Conservative.

SIR CHARLES PETRIE...

HON. J F RENNEL RODD, heir to Baron Rennell, and a partner in Morgan, Grenfell & Co.

RALPH D BLUMENFELD, Chairman of the Daily Express, formerly editor. He was once editor of the Daily Mail. He is the founder of the Anti-Socialist Union and a member of its Executive Committee.

It is significant that among the early supporters of Mosley are named a number of wealthy Jews. This was before Mosley adopted anti-semitism as an indispensable means of rallying ignorant and backward supporters.

Mosley had the financial backing of fascists abroad. He received a subsidy of £60,000 a year from Mussolini. This has been confirmed by the discovery of documents in the archives in Rome dated 1935, and was revealed by Chuter Ede, the Home Secretary, in the House of Commons.

Mosley paid visits to Hitler and Mussolini and was in close touch with the nazi leaders.

With the outbreak of the war, the Mosley movement declined. Like other fascist movements in Europe the BUF became an agent of German imperialism on whose victory they banked to assure their future. The British capitalists at war with German imperialism had no use for the fascists and were compelled to illegalise them as part of the ideological war against fascism. But Mosley was well protected in prison and pampered with many of the comforts to which he was accustomed, including the best foods, furniture and servants. As one of their class who had perhaps ventured too early, the British capitalists treated him solicitously with an eye to the future.

Are the British Capitalists Anti-Fascist?

The British capitalist class fought the war, not because they opposed fascism and what it represents, but in a desperate struggle against rival imperialisms for world markets, for sources of raw materials – for profit. Their victory has not brought and will not bring the end of fascism.

Throughout the world, the British ruling class has supported fascism and reaction against the progressive movements of the working class. Let us take but a few examples.

When Mussolini was subjecting the Italian working class to his castor oil "treatments" and other bestial tortures, Churchill became deeply impressed with his "gentle and simple bearing". Speaking in Rome on 20 January, 1927, Churchill found only praise for the fascists:

"I could not help being charmed, like so many other people have been, by Signor Mussolini's gentle and simple bearing and by his calm, detached poise in spite of so many burdens and dangers. Secondly, anyone could see that he thought of nothing but the lasting good, as he understood it, of the Italian people, and that no lesser interest was of the slightest consequence to him. If I had been an Italian I am sure that I should have been whole-heartedly with you from the start to finish in your triumphant struggle against the bestial appetites and passions of Leninism. I will, however, say a word on an international aspect of fascism. Externally, your movement has rendered service to the whole world. The great fear which has always beset every democratic leader or a working class leader has been that of being undermined by someone more extreme than he. Italy has shown that there is a way of fighting the subversive forces which can rally the masses of the people, properly led, to value and wish to defend the honour and stability of civilised society. She has provided the necessary antidote to the Russian poison. Hereafter no great nation will be unprovided with an ultimate means of protection against the cancerous growth of Bolshevism."

Here the outspoken mouthpiece of British capitalism clearly indicates that in the last resort, faced with the revolutionary working class, the "nation" (the capitalists) will not be "unprovided"; it will always be able to imitate Mussolini and adopt the fascist method of rule over the workers.

In the struggle of China against Japanese imperialism, the British backed Japan because they saw in her victory a bulwark against the rising struggles of the masses in Asia. Mr LS Amery, then Secretary of State for India, a position which he held right up till 1945, said on 27 February, 1933 in the House of Commons:

"I confess that I see no reason whatever why, either in act or in word, or in sympathy, we should go individually or intentionally against Japan in this matter. Japan has got a very powerful case based upon fundamental realities...Who is there among us to cast the first stone and to say that Japan ought not to have acted with the object of creating peace and order in Manchuria and defending herself against the continual aggression of vigorous Chinese nationalism? Our whole policy in India, our whole policy in Egypt, stand condemned if we condemn Japan."

The nazis were aided and financed by the British ruling class. Hitler received the unqualified approval and support of British big business. Lloyd George, the "Liberal", described Hitler as a "bulwark" against Bolshevism. As early as February 1934, the British government published a memorandum which allowed for an immediate increase in all German arms. "The German claim to equality of rights in the matter of arms cannot be resisted and ought not to be resisted. You will have to face rearmament of Germany," declared the British Foreign Secretary, Sir John Simon, on 6 February, 1934. Export to Germany of unwrought nickel, cotton waste, the basis for gun cotton, aircraft and tanks rose tremendously. When asked in March, 1934 if Vickers Ltd were engaged in rearming Hitler Germany, its chairman replied:

"I cannot give you an assurance in definite terms, but I can tell you that nothing is being done without complete sanction and approval of our own government." (Quoted by Henry Owen in *War is Terribly Profitable*)

The big financiers and bankers openly advocated a policy of support and assistance for Hitler. A short time after he came to power, the Governor of the Bank of England declared that loans to Hitler were justified as "an investment against Bolshevism".

Large loans were given to Hitler. His occupation of the Rhineland, the rearmament of Germany, the anschluss with Austria, the seizure of Czechoslovakia – all were supported by British capitalism. The reason: they feared a nazi collapse and what might replace it. Just before the war, the British, through RS Hudson, then Secretary of the Department of Overseas Trade, made an offer of a loan of a thousand million pounds to conciliate the nazis and prevent them from expanding at the expense of British imperialism while remaining a bastion against the German workers and against the working class throughout Europe.

Churchill looked upon the nazis with unbounded approval. In the 1939 edition of Great Contemporaries, Winston Churchill wrote about Hitler's rise to power:

"The Story of that Struggle cannot be read without admiration for the courage, the perseverance, the vital force which enabled him to challenge, defy, conciliate, or overcome, all authorities or resistance which barred his path...I have always said that if Great Britain were defeated in war, I hoped we should find a Hitler to lead us back to our rightful position among the nations." (The same book by Churchill contains a venomous attack on Trotsky, who earns his bitter hatred as builder of the Red Army and one of the leaders of the October revolution – EG)

Lord Beaverbrook, writing in the Daily Express on 31 October, 1938 said:

"We certainly credit Hitler with honesty and sincerity. We believe in his purpose stated over and over again, to seek an accommodation with us, and we accept to the full the implications of the Munich document."

This, of course, did not prevent him from holding ministerial office in the Coalition government in the "war against fascism".

In the Spanish civil war, the British capitalists were in sympathy with Franco. Under the cover of so-called "non-intervention" they assisted him to crush the Republic.

No reactionary anti-working class movement went unsupported and unaided by British capitalism. Only when the nazis encroached on their preserves did they declare war in the name of "anti-fascism". But when the needs of their class are such that fascism becomes necessary, they will as readily turn to Mosley or some other fascist adventurer, just as the German capitalists turned to Hitler and the Italian to Mussolini. Today, the fascists are not necessary for the defence of their profits. But tomorrow...

What is Fascism and How Does it Arise?

Most important for anti-fascists and working people is an understanding of fascism and why it arises. Without such an understanding of fascism it is not possible to effectively combat and destroy it. And unless it is viewed from the angle of the class structure of capitalist society and the class forces at work, the workers cannot prepare themselves for the future struggle against any rising fascist movement.

Capitalism as a system of society developed out of the decay of feudalism. In the period of its rise, up to the outbreak of the first world war, it was a progressive system because it resulted in the development of the forces of production, i.e. the power of man over nature, and consequently raised the level of culture of mankind.

Despite crises, wealth increased and in the main capitalist countries, the standards and the culture of the masses rose. With the development of technique the increased productivity of labour resulted in a further expansion of industry at the expense of the older methods of production and with this a numerical increase of the working class.

During the past 100 years, in their fight against capitalism, the working class organised their own class organisations, the trade unions and labour parties. It must always be remembered that the rights of today – the right to withhold labour – to strike, to organise, the right of free speech and press and even the right to vote, were not handed down benevolently by the capitalist class: these were won only after a bitter and ceaseless class struggle on the part of the workers. Before the first world war, the capitalists could still afford to give concessions from the enormous profits which the expansion of capitalism and imperialism brought them.

But capitalism inevitably brings in its train the concentration of capital and the growth of monopoly and of the combines. Because of the development of the world market, which is the historical function of the capitalist system, at a certain stage the capitalist nations inevitably and necessarily come into conflict with each other in the frantic endeavour to find and extend markets. The development of the productive forces expands more rapidly than the markets, outstrips the boundaries of the national state and private ownership of the means of production. It is this contradiction that led to the first world war, as it led to the second.

Capitalism in its last stages not only reduces the working class, which it cannot provide with any security in either employment or sustenance, to the state of pauperism; it ruins also the middle class – small shopkeepers and businessmen, professional people, white collar workers, small traders and all those strata of the population whose social position is lodged between the industrial working class and the capitalist class.

To combat the working class it is not possible for the capitalists to rely only on the old forces of repression embodied in the state machine. In modern conditions no state can last very long which does not, at least in its initial stages, possess a mass basis. A military police dictatorship does not serve the purpose. The capitalists find a way out in fascism which finds its mass support in the middle class on the basis of anti-capitalist demagogy. It is important to understand that fascism represents a mass movement: that of the disillusioned middle class.

The working class, in times of crisis, seek to express their aspirations and struggle through their existing organisations. Joined together by production, organised as a class in large factories and plants, the workers think in terms of a socialist solution to their problems. Their social position gives rise to a social consciousness.

The middle class, because of their position in society, wedged half-way between the capitalists and the workers, sway between these classes. If the working class cannot show a revolutionary way out for the middle class, the latter turns to the capitalist class and becomes the main pillar of support for the fascist movement.

With the increasing rivalry on the world market, unable to secure their position while the organisations of the working class exist, the capitalists seek a way out of the crisis by the destruction of these organisations, thereby depriving the workers of the weapons through which they defend their rights and conditions. As the crisis affects one country after another, the capitalists look to fascist movements to smash the working-class organisations and parties. Herein lies the function of fascism.

The difference between capitalist democracy and fascism is explained thus by Leon Trotsky:

"After fascism is victorious finance capital gathers into its bands as in a vice of steel, directly and immediately all the organs and institutions of sovereignty, the executive administrative and educational powers of the state: the entire state apparatus together with the army, the municipalities, the universities, the schools, the press, the trade unions and the co-operatives. When a state turns fascist it does not only mean that the forms and methods of government are changed in accordance with the patterns set by Mussolini – the changes in this sphere ultimately play a minor role but it means first of all for the most part, that the workers' organisations are annihilated; that the proletariat is reduced to an amorphous state and that a system of administration is created which penetrates deeply into the masses and which serves to frustrate the independent crystallisation of the proletariat. Therein precisely is the gist of fascism." (What Next? The Key Question for Germany, 1932)

Mussolini's Rise to Power

Fascism first appeared in Italy. At the end of the great world war of 1914-1918, the Italian ruling class became terrified at the revolutionary upsurge of the masses. The capitalist newspapers wrote that the workers and peasants of Italy were behaving as if Lenin and Trotsky were masters of Italy. A whole series of strike struggles took place - 1,663 in 1919; 1,881 in 1920. The workers forced concessions and reforms; better wages; the 8-hour day; general recognition of the trade unions; and a voice in production through factory committees. In September 1920, when the industrialists resorted to a lock-out as a reply to the demand for increased wages, 600,000 Italian metal workers occupied the mills and carried on production themselves, through their own elected shop committees.

The peasantry too were affected by the general revolutionary postwar wave. They began the seizure of the land. The Liberal Government was forced to give them the right to remain on the land they had spontaneously seized, on condition that they organised themselves into cooperatives. The agricultural labourers formed strong unions known as the "Red Leagues".

The capitalists and landowners were paralysed. Power was in the grasp of the working class. The ruling class manoeuvred in face of the onslaught of the masses, and began to seek a way out, planning a counter-offensive.

At the beginning of April 1919, in Genoa the big industrialists. and landowners formed an alliance for the fight against "Bolshevism". "This gathering," wrote Rossi (the anti-Fascist later murdered by Mussolini's agents) in his book *La Naissance du Fascisme*, "is the first step towards the reorganisation of capitalist forces to meet the threatening situation." After the formation of national General Federation of Industry, and a General Federation of Agriculture, the capitalists commenced to subsidise the Fasci, or aimed hooligan bands of Benito Mussolini.

This band was a specially trained anti-labour militia whose object was to terrorise the workers and at that stage, to disrupt their organisations. These anti-labour leagues began, openly, to attack meetings of workers. In Milan, stronghold of the Socialists, as early as April 15, 1919, a demonstration and march of Socialists including women and children, was attacked by the Fasci who were armed with daggers and hand grenades. In groups of two or three dozens, they attacked peaceful demonstrations of workers all over Italy. On the same day as the Milan episode, the offices of the official Italian Socialist paper, Avanti, were sacked by the fascists. On December 1, 1919, the Socialist deputies were attacked and beaten as they left the Houses of Parliament.

But the failure of the working-class to take power enabled the capitalists to undermine the gains the workers had made, and the aggravated crisis in Italy made the ruined middle class easy victims of fascist demagogy. Because of the smallness and unimportance of the Jewish population in Italy, anti-semitism was not part of the arsenal of Italian fascism. Their demagogy centred on opposition to the trusts and support for the little man. To the thugs and adventurers in Mussolini's militia, were added desperate students, unemployed, professional people and middle-class recruits generally.

The revolutionary energies of the masses ebbed. The fascists, lavishly financed by the big industrialists and landowners, began a real offensive against the workers. In Bologna, centre of Emilia's "Red

Leagues", the municipal elections in November 1920, brought a victory for the Socialist Party. On November 21, the Blackshirts attacked the town hall, and in the struggle a reactionary councillor was killed. (It appeared as if he had been killed by a fascist gunman.) This was the signal which the fascists had been awaiting. According to Gorgolini, one of Mussolini's supporters, this "opened the great fascist era...the law of brutal retaliation, atavistic and savage, reigned in the Peninsula. It was the will of the fascists."

In the villages, armed by the landowners and supplied with cars, the Blackshirts began punitive expeditions. Having wrecked the organisations of the workers in the villages, they now began to attack the workers in the towns. In 1921, in Trieste, Medina, Florence, and elsewhere, the Blackshirts wrecked the Labour Exchanges and the offices of the Cooperative and Labour newspapers.

Backing of the Capitalist State - Police, Law Courts and Army

In their offensive against the working class the Blackshirt thugs had the full backing of the forces of the capitalist state machine. The police recruited for the fascists, urging the criminal elements to join them, on the promise of all sorts of benefits and immunities. While the police placed their cars at the disposal of the fascists, and while giving permits to them to bear arms, they persistently refused applications for arms by workers and peasants. A fascist student sent a jeering letter to a communist paper, in which he wrote

"We have the police disarm you before we advance against you, not out of fear of you whom we despise, but because our blood is precious and should not be wasted against vile and base plebeians." (Rossi, ibid.)

Meanwhile, the "impartial" courts of law, handed out "centuries in prison sentences to the anti-fascists, and centuries of absolution for the guilty fascists." (Gobetti, *La Revolution Liberale*). In 1921, the Minister of Justice, Fera, "sent a communication to the magistrates asking them to forget about the cases involving fascist criminal acts." (Rosenberg, *Der Weltkampf des Fascismus*.)

The army, through its officer caste, backed the fascists to the hilt.

"General Badoglio, Chief of Staff of the Italian Army, sent a confidential circular to all commandants of military districts stating that the officers then being demobilised (there were about 60,000 of them) would be sent to the most important centres and required to join the fascists, which they would staff and direct. They would continue to receive four-fifths of their pay. Munitions from the State

Arsenals came into the hands of the fascist bands, which were trained by officers on leave, or even on active service. Many officers knowing the sympathies of their superiors had been won over to fascism, openly adhered to the movement. Cases of collusion between the army and the Blackshirts grew more and more frequent. For instance, the Fascio of Trent broke a strike with the help of an infantry company, and the Bolzano Fascio was founded by officers of the 232nd Infantry." (Daniel Guérin, *Fascism and Big Business*)

Within a short space of time, becoming bolder and bolder, the Blackshirts started a campaign to annihilate the workers' organisations. Malaparte – a fascist "theoretician" – related in his Technique du Coup-d'Etat, 1931, that: "Thousands of armed men, sometimes fifteen or twenty thousand, poured into a city or villages borne rapidly in trucks from one province to another." Daniel Guérin comments:

"Every day, they attacked the Labour Exchanges and the headquarters of cooperatives and working-class publications. In the beginning of August 1922, they seized the city halls of Milan and Leghorn which had socialist administrations, they burned the offices of the newspaper Avanti in Milan, and Lavoro in Genoa; they occupied the port of Genoa, stronghold of the dockworkers' labour cooperatives. Such tactics gradually wore out and weakened the organised proletariat, depriving it of its means of action and support. The fascists only waited for the conquest of power to crush it once and for all."

How did the workers' organisations face up to this mortal threat to their very existence? Instead of explaining the nature of fascism to the workers and what it would mean to them if Mussolini came to power, the leaders persisted in deluding themselves and their followers that the capitalist state would protect them from the menace of these lawless bands. Guérin relates how

"the Socialist and Union leaders obstinately refused to reply to fascism blow for blow, to arm and organise themselves in military fashion. 'Fascism cannot in any case be conquered in an armed struggle, but only in a legal struggle,' insisted Battaglia Syndicale for January 29, 1921. As they possessed contacts in the state apparatus, the socialists on several occasions were offered arms to protect themselves from the fascists. But they rejected these offers, saying that it was the duty of the state to protect the citizen against the armed attacks of other citizens.'" (Reference Kurella, *Mussolini ohne Maske*, 1931.)

The socialists even went to the extent of signing a peace pact with Mussolini on August 3, 1921. This, on the initiative of the Liberal Prime Minister and his statement that he desired to "reconcile" the socialists and fascists. Turati, leader of the socialists in Italy; appealed to Mussolini:

"I shall say to you only this: Let us really disarm!"

The Blackshirts must have laughed to themselves. They utilised this position the better to prepare. They denounced the pact and redoubled their offensive against the workers' organisations.

The socialists pleaded to the state to take action against the fascists. And the state took action. Raids were undertaken, not against the fascists, but against the workers and their organisations.

Because of the failure of the socialists and trade union leaders, left-wing militants of various tendencies – revolutionary trade unionists, left-wing socialists, young communists, socialists and republicans, with a few ex-Army officers organised armed anti-Fascist militias in 1921 on the initiative of Mingrino. They called themselves the "Arditi del Popolo". They undertook this in the teeth of the opposition of the labour and trade union leaders. Unfortunately, the young and weak Communist Party adopted an ultra-left attitude towards the problem. They split away and organised their own "Squadrons of Action".

"The result was," writes Guérin, "that when the Blackshirts undertook a 'punitive expedition' against a locality and attacked the headquarters of labour organisations or the 'red' municipalities, the militant workers were either incapable of resisting or offered an improvised, anarchic resistance that was generally ineffective. For the most part, the aggressor remained master of the field..."

Guérin writes further:

"After a 'punitive expedition', the anti-fascists abstained from reprisals, respected the 'fascists' residences, and launched no counter-attacks. They were satisfied with proclaiming 'general protest strikes'. But these strikes, intended to force the authorities to protect labour organisations against the fascist terror, resulted only in ridiculous parleys with the authorities who were in reality the accomplices of fascism. (Silone, Der Fascismus, 1934) As these strikes were unaccompanied by direct action, they left the enemy's forces intact. On the other hand, the fascists profited by the strikes to redouble their violence. They protected 'scabs', served as strike-breakers themselves, and 'in that threatening vacuum a strike creates around itself, dealt swift and violent blows at the heart of the enemy organisations.' (Malaparte, *Technique du Coup d'Etat*, 1931) However on the rare occasions when the anti-fascists offered an organised resistance to fascism, they temporarily got the upper hand. For instance, in Parma, in August 1922, the working-class population successfully checked a fascist attack in spite of the concentration of several thousand militiamen 'because the defence was organised in accordance with military methods' under the direction of the Arditi del Popolo." (A. Rossi, *La Naissance du Fascism*, 1938)

As the intention of the fascists to seize power became more and more obvious, Turati, the Socialist spokesman, appealed to the King in July, 1922, to "remind him that he is the supreme defender of the Constitution." Meanwhile, the capitalists had come to their own conclusions. Rossi writes of

"some very lively conferences that took place between Mussolini...and the heads of the General Federation of Industry, Sig. Benni and Olivetti. The chiefs of the Banking Association, who had paid out 20 millions to finance the March on Rome, the leaders of the Federation of Industry and the Federation of Agriculture, telegraphed Rome that, in their opinion, the only possible solution was a Mussolini government."

Senator Ettore Conti, a big power magnate, sent a similar telegram. "Mussolini was the candidate of the plutocracy and the trade associations."

Despite the fact that the fascists only had 35 deputies in the Italian Parliament out of about 600 or so, the King, obedient to the demands of the ruling classes, handed power to Mussolini.

Even after the coup of Mussolini in 1922, the reformist leaders were incapable of drawing the lessons from their bitter experiences.

"The Italian Socialists, blind as ever, continued to cling to legality and the Constitution. In December, 1923, the Federation of Labour sent Mussolini a report of the atrocities committed by fascist bands and asked him to break with his own troops. (Reference: Buozzi and Nitti, Fascisme et Syndicalisme, 1930) The Socialist Party took the electoral campaign of April, 1924, very seriously; Turati even had a debate at Turin with a fascist in a hall where Black Shirts guarded the entrance. And when, after Matteotti's assassination, a wave of revolt swept over the peninsula, the socialists did not know how to exploit it. 'At the unique moment,' Nenni writes, 'for calling the workers into the streets for insurrection, the tactic prevailed of a legal struggle on the judicial and parliamentary plane.' As a gesture of protest, the opposition was satisfied not to appear in parliament, and, like the ancient plebeians, they retired to the Aventine. 'What are our opponents doing?' Mussolini mocked in the chamber. Are they calling general strikes, or even partial strikes? Are they trying to provoke revolts in the army? Nothing of the sort. They restrict themselves to press campaigns.' (Speech, July 1924) The Socialists launched the triple slogan: Resignation of the Government, dissolution of the militia, new elections. They continued to display confidence in the

King, whom they begged to break with Mussolini; they published, for his enlightenment, petition after petition. But the King disappointed them a second time." (D. Guérin, Ibid.)

Conditions of life under Mussolini

Once in power, Mussolini, established the model totalitarian state. Having smashed the organisations of the workers, the way was prepared for a savage attack on the standards of the masses in the interests of Big Business. The main brunt of fascism was borne by the working class, against whom it is aimed above all. With their weapons of struggle broken, with the establishment of scab company unions, the conditions were created to drive down the wages and lower the standards of living of the workers. The Labour unions were crushed. Shop stewards' representation in the factories was abolished. The right to strike ended. All Union contracts were rendered void. The employer reigned supreme in the factories once again. He became at the same tune, the "leader" of his employees. Any attempt to strike, any resistance to the wishes of the employer, was "punished with ferocious, penalties by the State. To challenge the employer was to challenge the full force of the State. In the words of the fascists: strikes are crimes "against the social community..."

The anti-fascist Liberal, Gaetano Salvmini, an authority on Italy, who made a conscientious research into all aspects of life under fascism, basing himself on official fascist government sources, was enabled to show what fascism meant to the Italian people. In his book, Under the Axe of Fascism, he revealed that from the very beginning of the Mussolini regime the conditions of the people deteriorated, especially of the unfortunate workers and small peasants. In times of "prosperity" as well as during the depths of the slump of 1929-33, there were steady cuts in wages. The hours of work were steadily lengthened without any increase in overtime pay, while the cost of living increased. Giving extensive details of cuts in wages from 1922 right up till 1935, despite all the efforts of the regime to conceal this from the outside world, he shows how the consumption of the necessities of life steadily decreased.

In the year 1922, with a population of 38,800,000 the consumption of tobacco was 279,000 quintals; by 1932, it had fallen to 245,000 quintals. The consumption of coffee was 472,000 quintals in 1922 and fell in 1932 to 407,000 quintals. These are "luxuries" for the workers. But in the barest necessities of life, the fall was correspondingly great. Consumption of maize dropped from 27,213,000 quintals to 26,739,000 quintals in 1932. Consumption of wheat fell – and this with an increase in population to 41,000,000 in

1932 - from 72,237,000 quintals to 69,204,000 quintals. Salt, which, together with the above is absolutely essential to the barest minimum of existence, fell from 2,646,000 to 2,606,000 quintals. These figures are taken from official Italian statistics. (The Annuario Statistico Italiano for 1922-1925 page 198, and for 1933, page 119.) The Tribuna of May 1, 1935, revealed a terrible fall in the consumption of meat. "The annual consumption of meat, which in 1928 was 22 kilograms (48.4 pounds) per each member of the population (annually) had by 1932 declined to 18 kilograms (39.6 pounds). The consumption of sugar which rose to 7.5 kilograms in 1922 dropped to 6.9 in 1932. In England the annual consumption was 40 kilograms, in France 25, Germany 23, and even in backward Spain, 13 kilograms.

The official unemployment figures in Italy in February of 1933 were 1,229,000. On July 2, 1934, an official communiqué of the Italian Government informed us that "in the winter of that year 'national solidarity' in Italy gave help 'almost every day to 1,750,000 families'." In February 1922 there were only 602,000 unemployed, and the fascists centred a great deal of their demagogy on the horrors of unemployment.

Thus, the myth that fascism can avoid the crises of capitalism is shown to be a fraud.

Once in power, fascism retains its grip for a long period because of the shattering of the working class organisations. With all the best fighters, the most advanced proletarians in jail or murdered, the working class undergoes a period of demoralisation and apathy. Under the regime of repression and terror, the workers suffer under the greatest disadvantage for a unified struggle against the employers. The inglorious end of Mussolini was a demonstration to the world of the real hatred of the Italian people for the Duce, and an exposure of the lie that the Italian masses supported the Black Shirts.

Italian workers and fascism today

It is striking to note the difference between events in Italy after the second world war and the first.

Mussolini's fall was the signal for a deep-seated upsurge of the workers and peasants. Once again a tremendous wave of strikes and demonstrations followed the coup of Badoglio. And after the defeat of the Nazis, the workers and peasants, armed in their partisan detachments, repeated the process of taking over the factories and the control of the country. One thing stood in the path of the workers taking power: the leaders of their own organisations.

This failure has meant for the Italian workers a deterioration of their conditions to a level even lower than existed under Mussolini.

The workers have been able to defend themselves to a certain extent, because of the powerful unions they have constructed, far more powerful than in the past. But the middle class, ground down to standards even below that of the workers, has provided a favourable basis for the revival of fascist demagogy. They contrasted the promises of the capitalist democrats with their lot. The neo-fascists began to emerge. Armed with the experience of Mussolini's rise to power, the industrialists and land-owners proceeded on familiar lines. A May Day meeting in 1947 in Sicily was fired on, despite the fact that women and children were participating. In Naples some months before, bands of Monarchists and fascists demonstrated against the Communist Party and other workers' organisations. In the last few months of 1947 workers' meetings were fired on and bombs thrown at premises of workers' organisations. The terror of the fascists was greater in the countryside of the backward South, where the landowners organised the murder of trade union organisers and attempted to terrorise the agricultural workers and peasants against joining the unions.

Within a few months 19 trade union organisers were assassinated in the agricultural districts of the South.

In the North, even in such working class strongholds as Milan, bombs have been placed in the headquarters of the Communist Party. The workers swiftly replied by a general strike in Milan, and immediately took reprisal action against the headquarters of the neo-fascist organisations, l'Uomo Qualunque and Movimento Sociale Italiene, which were set on fire and sacked.

Having had experience of fascism, the Italian workers have not been content to remain on the defensive. In nearly all cities, big and small, they have gone on the offensive against the fascists. Demonstrations of over a hundred thousand in Milan, tens of thousands in other cities – Turin, Genoa, Florence, Verona, Bari, Cremona, Rome, Bologna, even in Naples and Palermo (former strongholds of reaction) the workers have made militant attacks on the headquarters of the fascist organisations. The backward South has followed the lead of the North.

Naturally, the police, always conveniently absent or inactive when the fascists have attacked the workers, have been called out to protect the fascists. Troops have been called out in many towns to assist the police. Tear gas and firearms have been used against the workers.

In this situation the de Gasperi Government, like its liberal predecessor of 1920-22 has surreptitiously given assistance and encouragement to the fascists. History repeats itself, but not exactly in the same way. The offensive of the workers led to the defeat of the fascists, who for the time being have been forced to lie low. The workers of Britain can learn a valuable lesson from the recent offensive movement of the Italian workers.

But this lesson has been a purely negative one: If having learned the negative lessons of preventing the fascists from rearing their heads, the workers fail to apply a positive solution, the menace of fascism even in Italy will not have been exorcised.

The chronic decay of capitalism in Italy continues. Already there is the mass unemployment of one and a half million workers. The first winds of the new world crisis will send unemployment soaring to record levels. Wracked by crises, the Italian capitalists will turn again to brutal suppression as the only means of stabilising their regime. The lesson of Italy must be learned above all by the vanguard of the working class movement. If they fail to show the alternative of the complete overthrow of the capitalist system and the establishment of workers' power and communism, the great offensive spirit of the masses will wane, and demoralisation and indifference will set in. Capitalism breeds fascism; the workers can guarantee the end of fascism only by overthrowing the capitalist system of society.

Germany - How the Nazis came to power

The defeat of the German working class, on the coming to power of Hitler, set the world workers' movement back for many years. In tracing the background to the events in Germany, we can see clearly the class forces at work, the role of the German Social Democrats and Stalinists which led to the terrible defeat of one of the most powerfully organised labour movements in the world.

In the wake of the Russian revolution, the German working class overthrew the Kaiser and attempted a revolutionary overthrow of capitalism in 1918.

But it was the German Social Democrats who came to power, though they had actually opposed the insurrection and the revolution.

They had no intention of consummating the revolution. Their pro-gramme was based on "the inevitability of gradualism". Having raised themselves above the level of the workers, they had abandoned the Marxist programme on which their party had been based for decades. Noske, Ebert, Schiedemann, the leaders of the Social Democracy – conspired with the German General Staff to destroy the revolution and restore "law and order". The Berlin workers were shot down in January, 1919, and the revolutionary leaders – Luxemburg and Liebknecht were murdered by reactionary officers on the direct instigation of the Social Democratic leaders. The Soviets established in the revolution were eliminated, and Germany became a democratic capitalist state – the most democratic in the world, according to the boast of the Social Democrats.

At this stage the capitalists were compelled to lean on the Labour and Trade Union leaders in order to save their system from complete collapse. Grinding their teeth, they were forced to make tremendous concessions to the working class. The workers won the eight-hour day, trade union recognition, unemployment insurance, the right to elect shop committees, and universal suffrage for men and women. The agricultural labourers who lived under semi-feudal conditions in East Prussia under the Junkers, won the right to organise and similar rights to those of the industrial workers.

Recovering from the first shock, the big industrialists and landowners began to prepare for the offensive against the working class. Their attitude was exemplified by that of Krupp, the armament magnate who arrogantly informed his workers: "We want only loyal workers who are grateful from the bottom of their hearts for the bread which we let then earn." By February 1919, Stinnes, another of the iron and steel magnates of the Ruhr was declaiming openly: "Big business and all those who rule over industry will some day recover their influence arid power. They will be called back by a disillusioned people, half dead with hunger, who will need bread and not phrases." The former Minister, Dernberg, representative of big industry, declared openly: "Every eight-hour day is a nail in Germany's coffin."

Already in these early years, the capitalists began to finance anti-labour leagues composed of ex-army officers, criminals, adventurers and other social riff-raff. The Nazis were at this time, one small anti-labour grouping among others.

They commenced a campaign of terror, which included assassinations of left-wing, and even capitalist democratic politicians. They commenced a campaign of breaking up working class meetings. "The National Socialist movement will in the future prevent, if need be by force, all meetings or lectures that are likely to exercise a depressing influence..." declared Hitler on January 4, 1921. As in Italy, so in Germany, the courts, the army authorities, the civil service, the heads of the police, gave every support to these reactionary groups. The State acted in complicity and in collusion with them. When the Munich Chief of Police, Pohner, was warned of the existence of "veritable organisations of political assassination", he replied : "Yes, yes, but too few!"

But at this stage, these fascist groups had no mass base. They comprised an insignificant social force, composed only of the dregs of society. The middle class looked to the workers' organisations to show a way out. The capitalists used the fascist organisations only as anti-labour auxiliaries, and a reserve for the future. Dealing with the development of. the Nazi movement, Hitler admitted: "Only one thing could have broken our movement – if the adversary had understood its principles and from the first day had smashed, with the most extreme brutality, the nucleus o f our new movement." Goebbels remarked: "If the enemy herd known how weak we were, it would probably have reduced us to jelly...It would have crushed in blood the very beginning of our work."

In the revolutionary crisis of 1923, caused by the inflation and the occupation of the Ruhr by France, the middle class looked towards the Communist Party which had succeeded in gaining the support of the majority of the workers. But the revolutionary situation was bungled by the then leaders of the German Communist Party, Brandler and Thalheimer, and by the wrong advice given by Stalin in Moscow to the leadership of the Communist Party.

Brandler admitted subsequently at a meeting of the Executive Committee of the Communist International:

"There were signs of a rising revolutionary movement. We had temporarily the majority of the workers behind us, and in the situation believed that under favourable circumstances we could proceed immediately to the attack..."

After the possibility of seizing power had been lost, the leadership of the International tried to put all the responsibility on the shoulders of the German Party. But the German leaders had looked for advice to the leadership of the Communist International in Moscow. Stalin's advice was catastrophic. He wrote to Zinoviev and Bukharin at that time:

"Should the Communists strive to seize power without the Social Democrats, are they mature enough for that? That, in my opinion is the question...Of course, the Fascists are not asleep, but it is to our interest that they attack first: that will rally the whole working class around the Communists (Germany is not Bulgaria). Besides, according to all information the Fascists are weak in Germany. In my opinion the Germans must be curbed and not spurred on."

This, when they had the majority of the workers behind them! Thus tragically the German revolution was ruined and the basis laid for a subsequent increase in fascist influence.

Big Business and the Nazis

Scared by the perspective of "Bolshevism" in Germany, the American, British and French capitalists poured in loans to prop up German capitalism. These loans resulted in a capitalist boom on a world scale, which particularly affected Germany. The boom in

Germany lasted from 1925 until 1929. The capitalists of Germany coining enormous profits out of the rationalisation of German industry, did not need the fascists, and the support for the Nazis declined. They received only sufficient funds to keep them in existence as a reserve weapon and to prevent their disappearance from the scene altogether.

Then came the world slump of 1929-33. The workers' standards, of living dropped. Unemployment rose to seven millions and more. The middle class were ruined in the economic crisis, and they found their standards dropping lower than the levels of the working class. The industrial workers had the protection of their union contracts and unemployment allowances within limits, and could thus resist the worst impositions of the combines and monopolies. But the middle class was helpless.

The industrialists were alarmed at the prospect of proletarian revolution. They now began to pour fabulous sums into the coffers of the Nazi Party. Krupp, Thyssen, Kirdorff, Borsig, the heads of the coal, steel, chemical and other industrial empires in Germany, supplied Hitler lavishly with the means of propaganda. The final decision to hand power over to Hitler was taken at the home of the Cologne banker, Schroder, (who, according to the Nazi racial laws was a Jew!) Enormous subsidies such as no other political party in Germany had ever received, were rained upon the Nazis by the capitalists. They considered the time had come to destroy the organisations and rights of the working class.

Explaining what the subsidies meant, Hitler pointed out that:

"Without automobiles, airplanes and loud speakers, we could not have conquered Germany. These three technical means enabled National Socialism to carry on an amazing campaign..."

In a confidential document published by the British Government in 1943, for the use of officials and civil servants who were to be sent to Germany, the following irrefutable facts are given:

"Fritz Thyssen and Kirdorff in the Ruhr, and Ernst von Borsig in Berlin, chairman of the German Employers' Federation (Vereinigung Deutscher Arbeitgeberverbande) were the extreme supporters of Hitler...Among other financial supporters of earlier Hitler days were the famous piano manufacturers, Karl Bechstein, Berlin, the printer Bruckmann (Munich), the well-known art dealer and publisher, Hanfstaengl (Munich), and the Reetsma Cigarette combine in Hamburg which, after Hitler came to power was granted an exclusive monopoly.

"But it was not only during the big crisis preceding the Nazi government that financial support by great industrial corporations began on a larger scale. Most of these did not give their contributions to the Nazi party direct, but to Alfred Hugenberg, the former director of Krupps and leader of the 'Deutschnationale Volkspartei' (German National People's Party). Hugenberg placed one-fifth of the amount given at the disposal of the NSDAP...

"Fritz Thyssen, since his break with Hitler, has stated that his personal contribution amounted to one million Rm., and he estimated the amount the NSDAP received from Heavy Industry via Hugenberg at about two million Rm. annually.

"At the meeting of the Dusseldorf Club of industrialists on January 27, 1932, after Hitler had enlightened them about his programme, the pact between the heavy industry and the Nazi party was sealed. Here Hitler convinced his audience that they had nothing to fear from his 'socialism', and then he commended himself with his semi-military organisation as the bulwark against any kind of 'Bolshevism'.

"The economic policy carried on by the 'National-Socialists' nevertheless completely justified the confidence which the big industrialists had placed in Hitler. Hitler has in every other respect carried out their policy. He has destroyed the workers' organisations. He has introduced the 'leadership principle' in the factories. He has brought about an expansion of heavy industry in Western Germany by means of an immense rearmament programme and has brought the firms enormous profits. The profits which the manufacturers of the Ruhr and Rhineland were able to make are dearly shown in the so-called 'Decree' regarding the surrender of 'dividends' of 1941. (*Dividend en abgabeverordnung*). This Decree, which like so many Nazi Decrees, means the opposite of what its name indicates, enabled the joint stock companies to realise profits which they had accumulated during 1933-38 and which had not been paid out in dividends by way of so-called 'rectification'. About 5,000,000,000 Rms. of accumulated profits, which had been made in the pre-war years were distributed to the shareholders in the form of bonus shares."

Trotsky Calls for the United Front

In the General Election of May 1924, the Nazis received 1,920,000 votes with 32 deputies. But in December of the same year, after the Dawes Plan had restored some stability to German economy, they received 840,000 and the decline of the Nazis went even further. In the elections for the German President in 1925, General Ludendorff, the candidate of the Nazis obtained 210,000! In the General Election of May 1928, the Nazis received only 720,000 votes, losing 120,000 votes and two seats.

Then came the world slump and the frightful crisis of German capitalism. Within two years at the General Election of September 14, 1930, the Nazi vote rose to 6,000,000. The fascists had drawn to their banner large sections of the despairing middle class. The failure of the Socialists in 1918 and of the Communists in 1923 had driven a formidable proportion of the middle class from neutrality or even support of the workers, to the side of the counter-revolution with its denunciation of "Marxism", i.e., Socialism.

Immediately the elections results were known, Trotsky and the Left Opposition - who considered themselves a part of the Communist International although they had been expelled – issued an appeal to the German Communist Party to immediately organise a united front with the Social Democrats to prevent the coming to power of Hitler. Only thus could they hope to protect the rights of the working class from the threat of the Nazis. The Trotskyists warned of the tragic consequences which the coming to power of the Nazis could mean, not only to the German, but to the whole international working class movement. They warned that it would make war against the Soviet Union inevitable.

But the Stalinists took no heed. Their policy in Germany was that fascism or "social fascism" was already in power; that the main danger to the working class was Social Democracy, who were also fascists - "social-fascists".

The British Trotskyists were expelled from the Communist Party in 1932 for advocating the united front between Social Democrats and Communists in Germany as well as in Britain.

"It is significant," wrote the British Stalinists in the Daily Worker of May 26, 1932, "that Trotsky has come out in defence o f a united front between the Communist and Social Democratic Parties against Fascism. No more disruptive and counter-revolutionary class lead could possibly have been given at a time like the Present."[46]

---

[46] This line was not confined to Germany. The tiny Communist Party of Britain advocated the break-up of Labour Party meetings. Pollitt wrote in the *Daily Worker*, on January 29, 1930: "There should not be a Labour meeting held anywhere, but what the revolutionary workers in that district attend such meetings and fight against the speakers, whoever they are, so-called 'left', 'right' or 'centre'. They should never be allowed to address meetings. This will bring us into conflict with the authorities but this must be done. The fight can no longer be conducted in a passive manner."

Ernst Thaelmann, in his closing speech at the 13th Plenum of the Communist International in September 1932 (see *Communist International*, No. 17/18, p. 1,329) said:

"In his pamphlet on the question, How Will National Socialism be Defeated?, Trotsky gives always but one reply: 'The German CP must make a bloc with the Social Democracy...' In framing this bloc, Trotsky sees the only way for completely saving the German working class against fascism. Either the CP will make a bloc with the social democracy or the German working class is lost for 10 to 20 years.

"This is the theory of a completely ruined fascist and counter-revolutionary. This theory is the worst theory, the most dangerous theory and the most criminal that Trotsky hay constructed in the last years of his counter-revolutionary propaganda."

The fountainhead of this policy of the German CP, Stalin, gave the line to the German Party.

"These two organisations [Social Democracy and National Socialism] are not mutually exclusive, but on the contrary are mutually complementary. They are not antipodes but twins. Fascism is a shapeless bloc of these two organisations. Without this bloc the bourgeoisie could not remain at the helm." (*Communist International*, No. 6, 1925)

The Stalinists even went to the extent of inciting Communist workers to beat up Socialist workers, break up their meetings, etc. Thaelmann openly put forward the slogan: "Chase the social fascists from their jobs in the plants and the trade unions." Following on the line, the organ of the Young Communists The Young Guard, propounded the slogan: "Chase the social fascists from the plants, the employment exchanges and the apprentice schools." Even the organ of the Young Pioneers, catering for the children of communists, the Drum called upon communists' children to "strike the little Zoergiebels in the schools and the playgrounds." (Zoergiebels was the Social Democratic chief of police.)

They did not stop there. The leaders of the Communist International went to the extent of advocating that the German CP unite with the Fascists against the Social Democrats. The Social Democratic Party was in power in Prussia which consisted of two-thirds, and the most important part, of Germany. There was a traditional saying in Germany: "He who has Prussia has the Reich." The Nazis organised a plebiscite on August 9, 1931, in an endeavour to throw the Social Democratic government out of office. Had they succeeded in this, they would have come to power in 1931 instead of 1933. The German CP leadership decided to oppose the referendum and support the Social Democrats. But the leadership of the

Comintern, under the direct influence of Stalin, demanded that the CP participate in this referendum and called it a "Red Referendum". At the Executive Committee of the Communist International, Piatnitzky even boasted:

"You know, for example, that the leadership of the Party opposed taking part in the referendum on the dissolution of the Prussian Landtag. A number of Party newspapers published leading articles opposing participation in that referendum. But when the Central Committee of the Party jointly with the Comintern arrived at the conclusion that it was necessary to take an active part in the referendum the German comrades in the course of a few days roused the whole Party. Not a single party, except the CPSU could do that..."

It was mad adventures of this character which disoriented the workers and facilitated the success of the Nazis. The refusal of the leaders of the mass workers' organisations to carry out a revolutionary policy against the fascists, resulted in this mighty working class movement, with a Marxist tradition of 75 years, being smashed and rendered impotent before the Nazi thugs.

It is important to bear in mind that the Nazis won only a small percentage of the German workers; the overwhelming majority were opposed to them. In 1931, the Nazis obtained only 5% of the votes in the elections for the shop committees in the factories. This was after a terrific campaign to penetrate the working class. And in March 1933, after the fascists were placed in power, despite the fact that the terror had already begun, they got only 3% of the votes in the elections for the shop committees! Despite the false policies of the leaderships, which led to a certain demoralisation within the ranks of the workers and helped the fascists' attempts to penetrate their ranks, the overwhelming majority of the workers remained faithful to the ideas of socialism and communism.

How Socialists and Communists faced Hitler threat

The workers were anxious and willing to fight the Nazis to prevent them coming to power. Millions were armed and trained in the Socialist and Communist Defence organisations. This was a legacy of the German revolution. The organised working class constituted the mightiest power in Germany... Had they only had the necessary policy to fight for the defence of their organisations and pass to the counter-offensive to take power. But the leaders betrayed the workers in Germany as they did in Italy.

As the danger of a Hitler coup grew closer, these misleaders declared that the Nazis were on the decline. The Socialist leaders declared, as if plagiarising their Italian counterparts: "Courage under unpopularity." They urged the necessity to support the decree laws of the Bruning Government, and to support Hindenburg as against the danger from Hitler. They scoffed at the idea that a highly civilised country like Germany could fall under the domination of fascist barbarism. Fascism could come to power in a backward country like Italy, but not Germany with its highly-industrialised economy! At first, they scoffed at the crudities and insane ideas put forward by the Nazis. They urged the workers to laugh at them and disregard their provocations. It only gives them publicity, they said. It can't happen here. We know the familiar arguments of middle-class intellectuals such as Rebecca West, in Britain and elsewhere.

Constantly they underestimated the danger from the fascists and appealed to the very state machine which was protecting and shielding the fascists.

But as the fascist menace loomed nearer, sections of the Socialist workers and the Trade Unions began to form defence groups in the factories and among the unemployed. But the German TUC, the Labour Federation, refused to support this: "...the situation [was] not sufficiently grave to justify the workers preparing for a struggle to defend their rights." It was opposed to "centralising and generalising these preventive measures", on the grounds that they were "superfluous". On November 6, 1932, Vorwarts, the central organ of the Social Democracy wrote of the fall in the poll for the Nazis from 13,700,000 to 11,705,257 and the refusal of Hindenburg to hand power to Hitler: "Ten years ago we predicted the bankruptcy of National Socialism; it is written in black and white in our paper!"

On the eve of the Nazis' accession to power, Schiffrin, one of the leaders of the Social Democrats wrote: "We no longer perceive anything but the odour of a rotting corpse. Fascism is definitely dead: it will never arise again."

The line of the leaders of the CP was, if anything, even worse. They declared that fascism was already in power in Germany and that the coming to power of Hitler would not make any difference. In the Reichstag, Remmele, one of their leaders, declared, on October 14, 1931: "Herr Bruning has put it very plainly once they [the Fascists] are in power, then the united front of the proletariat will be established and it will make a clean sweep of everything." (Violent applause from the communists.) "We are not afraid of the Fascist gentlemen. They will shoot their bolt quicker than any other government." ("Right you are!" from the communists.)

In 1932 Thaelmann, in a speech to the Central Committee, condemned "the opportunistic over-estimation of Hitler fascism." As early as the first victory of the Hitler movement at the polls in the

September 14, 1930, elections the central organ of the German CP Rote Fahne, declared: "September 14 was the culminating point of the National Socialist movement in Germany. It will be followed only by weakening and decline." Within three years, the Nazis had succeeded in winning the bulk of the middle class and obtaining over 13 million votes.

Just at the time when the Nazis received their first check at the polls and lost two million votes, and the signs of the disintegration of the Nazi movement appeared, President Hindenburg, the army leaders, the bureaucracy and the great industrialists and landowners handed power over to Hitler.

Even at the thirteenth hour, the Socialist and Stalinist leaders gave no righting lead. On February 7, 1933, Kunstler, head of the Berlin Federation of the Social Democratic Party, gave this instruction to the labour workers:

"Above all do not let yourselves be provoked. The life and health of the Berlin workers are too dear to be jeopardised lightly; they must be preserved for the day of struggle."

This when Hitler had already come to power, in January 1933.

The Communist Party leaders cried: "Let the workers beware of giving the Government any pretext for new measures against the Communist Party!" (Wilhelm Pieck, February 26, 1933)

The leaders of these parties did nothing even after Hitler carne to power. And the German workers wanted to fight. On March 5, the night of the elections, the heads of the Reichsbanner, the military organisation of the Social Democracy, asked for the signal for insurrection. They received the reply from the leaders of the Social Democratic Party: "Be calm! Above all no bloodshed." The mighty German Labour movement was surrendered to Hitler without a shot being fired.

The struggle for a united front by the Communist Party; the formation of such a united front of struggle in 1930, would have transformed the whole future course of events. The middle class would have followed the lead of the workers' organisations. Had the fascists been confronted with the organised might of the workers, they would have been smashed. Cravenly capitulating to the "authorities", the leadership allowed Hitler to score a very cheap victory.

The reformists and Stalinists are the same in all countries. In later years the responsibility for the debacle was shouldered onto the German workers. But at the Brighton Congress of the TUC, the Chairman, Citrine, defended the trade union leaders in Germany and their failure to call a general strike in 1933. He said:

"Shortly after the elections the campaign of terror developed. The Socialist movement and the Trade Union movement were virtually suppressed on May 2. There bad been a great deal of concern about the apparent absence of resistance to the advent of the Nazi dictatorship. German trade union leaders and German Socialist leaders were openly attacked and criticised on platforms because of the absence of effective resistance. All he could say was that he knew from first-hand knowledge that very adequate means of resistance were prepared...

"...All he could say was that a general strike was definitely planned and projected, but the German leaders had to give consideration to the fact that a general strike, after the atmosphere created by the Reichstag fire, and with six and a quarter million people unemployed at the least, was an act fraught with the gravest consequences, consequences which might be described as nothing less than civil war. He hoped they would never be put into a similar position in this country. He hoped they would never have to face that position." (The Menace of Dictatorship, page 8)

What happened to the middle class

The Nazis demagogically attacked the Jews, the Trusts and the Combines. They even proposed the break-up of big industry and its division among small businessmen and the break-up of the big department stores and their division among the shopkeepers. Of course they had no intention of carrying out these demagogic proposals, which in any case it would have been impossible to do. Thus, they gathered support among the middle class masses. This was the social base of the fascists.

Yet it was ironic that the middle class dupes of the Nazis were the strata of the population who suffered the worst once the Nazis had come to power. The Nazis had bewailed the dying out of the middle class, the most important strata of the nation, the backbone of the race. The statistics tell their own story of the crushing of small capital by the giant monopolies and combines. The tendency for the concentration of capital far from being slowed down, was speeded up because there was no means of resistance by the small man. And this process was consciously aided by the Nazis. In his book The Coming Crisis, Sternberg points out that in 1925 the number of proprietors in Germany, together with their dependants amounted to 12,027,000 persons, or 20.9% of the total population. Owing to the havoc of the crisis by the time the Nazis came to power in 1933, the total dropped to 11,247,000 or 19.8% of the total population. In the first 6 years of Nazi rule, in the period of Wehrwirhschaft (war economy) the number had declined still further to 9,612,000, or 16.2% of the total population.

The German economic publication *Wirtschaft und Statistik* of 1940 (page 336) brutally comments as follows on this phenomenon:

"The decline in the number of proprietors together with their dependants – their total was reduced by 1.7 millions or approximately 15% from 1933 – is in accordance with a long and steady trend of development. From 1895 onwards, their numbers have decreased from census to census, though the decline since 1933 is, of course, a record one."

Further evidence of this process is given in Germany, A Basic Handbook, which points out:

"The concentration of capital in fewer and fewer hands has proceeded rapidly. Many small and medium-sized firms have been absorbed by the big concerns. From 1937 to the end of 1942, the capital invested in joint stock companies increased by over 10 percent. At the same time, the total number of these companies decreased. Thus, at the end of 1942, one percent of the companies owned 60 percent of the capital invested in- joint stock companies. As the *Deutsche Allegemeine Zeitung*, January 6, 1944, points out: 'Of the total number of German joint stock companies with a capital of 30 milliard Rms., approximately three-quarters to four-fifths are owned by large shareholders or combines.'"

Representatives of Big Business were given all the key positions in the economy. At the same time there was "mutual interpenetration; on the one hand the leading industrialists, bankers, as leaders of the war economy, leaders of Gau (regions) Economic Chambers of Trade Groups...of Reich Associations, etc, became servants of the state, and were appointed to high administrative position's; on the other hand, high ranking officials, the Nazified bureaucracy of the State departments endeavoured to obtain highly-paid positions in the sphere of private enterprise. In the end, there were a number of semi-State, semi-private, companies which may be described as public utilities in the industrial sphere. The best known of this kind is the Hermann Goring-Concern."

"...It is quite obvious that this development gave ample opportunity to the Nazi elite to become the new Nazi industrialists and profiteers, and thus we see these new names, together with the old and well-known names of the various branches of German and Austrian industry, in the leading positions of the management and boards of the various branches of the Goring-Combine...

"In this connection, a few words may be added about a typical Party enterprise, Gustloff Foundation, which was founded on 'aryanised' property, the Suhl gun factory in Thuringia, in honour of Wilhelm Gustloff, a Nazi agent in Switzerland, who was shot in 1934, and which soon turned into a not unimportant machine-tool and armament combine, consisting of six companies, among them the famous Austrian Hirtenberg munitions factory. This combine is run solely by the Party, that is, by the Thuringen gauleiter Sauckel...Nothing is known of the finances of the Foundation since, like the Hermann Göring Werke, it does not publish balance sheets or profit and loss accounts.

"The development of this Party sector of Big Business does not constitute nationalisation, nor is it a negation of capitalism or plutocracy. On the contrary, it is the retention of all that enables Party members to build up for themselves industrial empires and to tap new sources of income.

"Thus, the ranks of the old rulers of industry and commerce lent themselves to a compromise so long as the benefits accruing from the alliance with the Party elite and bureaucracy, e.g. the joint spoilation of small enterprise and all strata of the 'little man' – outweigh all sacrifices by the group."

In the June 30, 1934 purge, Hitler struck against those elements in the ranks of the fascists who were demagogically playing on the aspirations of the middle class, as well as against those who had genuinely been deluded by the propaganda lies of the Nazis. Having accomplished this, Hitler transformed his dictatorship into a military-police state, representing the interests of the industrialists and landlords. Instead of the Junker estates being broken up and given to the peasants as promised, the power of the former was strengthened. Instead of breaking up the big department stores and dividing them among the small shopkeepers, instead of the abolition of the combines and monopolies, the small shops were closed down in thousands, and, a further concentration of the economy into the hands of the trusts took place.

From this we see that the only promise which was kept was the persecution of the unfortunate Jews. The middle class was despoiled, the workers organisations crushed, and only the high Nazi functionaries and Big Business benefited from Hitler rule. All the worst excesses of the capitalist system found expression because no opposition or the check of public opinion was allowed.

Reign of Terror

Once in power, the Nazis went ahead speedily, and accomplished in months what had taken the Italian fascists years. The political parties were illegalised; the trade unions were destroyed; the funds of the workers' organisations were confiscated for the benefit of the Nazis. The concentration camps were opened, and a reign of terror commenced against the working class Socialists and Communists, and Jews, such as had never been seen in modern history.

The fascists made great play of the fact that there was no unemployment under Hitler Germany. It is true that as a result of Hitler's immense rearmament plans, the forced labour on German arms and fortifications, there was no unemployment. Of course, had the war not intervened there would have been in Germany a disastrous economic slump as in other capitalist countries. Hitler spent fabulous sums in preparing for war which he saw as the only road for German imperialism and his own regime. He staked everything on armaments production on a scale never before reached in any state in peace time.

The German workers had to work long hours for low wages in order to prepare instruments of destruction which would be no benefit to them or to workers of other lands. They were employed...to produce for the terrible catastrophe that overtook Germany in the war. Hitler regarded them as pigs to be fattened for the slaughter.

In 1935, an employers' report enthusiastically hailed the new labour laws "at the present time, precisely, which requires increased intensification of production..." (that is, speed up). Goering openly declared in a speech: "We must work doubly hard today to lead the Reich out of decadence, impotence, shame and poverty. Eight hours a day is not enough. We must Work!" On May 22, 1933, Hitler said in the Reichstag: "In Germany private property is sacred."

Of all the 25 points of the Nazi "Programme" only the persecution of the Jews, a scapegoat for the crimes of capitalism, was carried out. The disillusionment was given an outlet in Jew-baiting. Even after they had been rendered helpless, deprived of all rights, thrown into concentration camps, the myth of the Jews being responsible for all the ills of society was fostered. As Hitler pointed out: if he had not had the Jews, he would have herd to invent them. No wonder Goebbels regretted publicly that the Nazis had ever published a programme.

After the war and the defeat of German imperialism, the Allies have not brought about the destruction of fascism. The middle class, the potential mass base for fascism, is today supporting the Christian Democrats of Germany. The Stalinist policy of reparations and revenge could not rally the support of the German masses. As a result of the policy of the Allies, the German masses are nearing literal starvation. When the slump hits Germany, the collapse of the "democratic" capitalist parties is inevitable. There is no middle road. The alternatives will be posed in Germany again: either the victory of the working class or a new fascist dictatorship.

Mosley Before the War and the Anti-fascist Struggles of the Workers

The laws of the decline of the capitalist system are the same in Britain as in other capitalist countries. The legend, assiduously cultivated, in particular by the leaders of the labour movement, that Britain is "different" has no basis in fact. This has been demonstrated on many occasions in the history of capitalist Britain. Fascism, as an expression of the decline of capitalist society can become under certain conditions as real a menace in Britain as it became in capitalist Germany and Italy.

The world slump of 1929-33 saw the emergence of the Mosley-fascist movement as a serious force for the first time in this country. The capitalist class of Britain recognised in the Mosley movement a militant and extra parliamentary weapon which they could utilise against the working class in a period of social upheaval, in times of crisis and slump. Only the fact that the British capitalists succeeded in emerging from those critical years without the need for direct action against the workers determined their limited use of fascists at that time. Nevertheless, they kept the fascist movement in being as an "insurance" against the future.

The myth, propagated by the capitalist class, that all issues can and will be settled through parliament is exploded by the very preparations undertaken by the capitalists themselves when it seemed possible that the working class would take to the road of struggle. With the threat of an economic slump looming before the war, the British capitalists were preparing extra-parliamentary steps against the working class.

In the few years before the war of 1939-45, army manoeuvres in Britain were conducted on the basis of civil war tactics. Strategic government buildings were prepared for defence. The civil guard was created as a special strike-breaking force, composed of recruits from the ranks of the ruling and upper middle class and trained in the use of machine-guns, rifles and tanks. They were taught to drive locomotives, heavy transport lorries and to do ground staff work at aerodromes. The civil guard was to constitute the backbone of any strike-breaking force in the event of serious troubles with the workers.

A significant portent was the fact that the big insurance companies which, together with the big banks, are the decisive rulers of Britain, refused to insure against the risk of civil disturbances and civil war. The capitalists understood that Britain, no more than Italy, France, Germany or Spain, could escape the social upheavals of the sick and decaying capitalist system. If the second world war had not intervened, the impending economic slump would have struck the country with far greater effect than even in 1929.

At this time the fascists were receiving support from numerous influential British industrialists. Towards the end of 1936 Mosley boasted in an interview with the Italian fascist paper *Giornale d'Italia*, that he was "receiving support from British industrialists". And that "a number of industrialists in the north who hitherto had given his movement secret support, fearing commercial boycott, are now stating openly that they are on the fascist side". (*News Chronicle*, 19 October, 1936) Mosley received the backing of the powerful newspapers, the *Daily Mail, Evening News* and the *Sunday Dispatch*.

Then as now, the blackshirt movement carried out its anti-working-class and anti-semitic provocations under the protection of the state. The British fascists were soon to prove that in brutality and method there was little to choose between them and Hitler's stormtroops or Mussolini's squadri. At a mass rally of British fascists at Olympia on 7 June 1934, the British working class were given an idea of what to expect if fascism triumphed. The savage and calculated brutalities inflicted by the specially trained fascist thugs upon any of the audience who dared to voice even the mildest opposition to Mosley's speech by interjections, outraged all sections of the population. Organised bands of fascists set upon hecklers, men and women alike, beating them unconscious, kicking them while on the ground.

Nurtured and aided by the authorities and the police, the fascists insolently organised provocative marches in working-class and Jewish districts, imitating the tactics of the nazis at the dawn of their movement in Germany. The British working class gave the blackshirts their answer. Every demonstration called by the fascists was answered by a great counter-demonstration of workers and anti-fascists. At Trafalgar Square, Hyde Park, in Liverpool, Merthyr, Newcastle - all over the country – the workers rallied against the fascists. In red Glasgow, the fascists were unable to hold meetings. In the working-class district of Bermondsey, London, barricades put up and manned by tens of thousands of workers successfully prevented the Mosley-fascists from marching through Long Lane.

Outstanding in these struggles of the workers against the fascists was the defeat of Mosley's projected march through the East End of London in 1936. Despite appeals from all sections of the working-class movement, including even the labour leaders, the then Home Secretary, Sir John Simon, refused to ban the march. On the contrary, he sought to facilitate it in every way. Ten thousand foot and mounted police drawn from all over London and the provinces were mobilised to protect Mosley and his 2500 fascists to ensure their march through the East End. This police protection was thoroughly organised even to the extent of wireless equipment and an autogiro hovering overhead. The weight of the state was brought to bear to protect the blackshirts in the teeth of the opposition of the London working class. The police authorities planned for Mosley's protection as though it were a military project.

Despite these measures of the state, the fascist march was defeated. Half a million workers turned out on the streets. Rallying around the slogan, "They Shall Not Pass", the workers formed a wall of bodies on the route through which Mosley was to march. From early morning, baton charges were made by the mounted police against the workers to clear a path for the fascists. But the determined opposition of the workers made it impossible. The police tried to create a diversion by clearing Cable Street. But here again, the workers of London threw up fresh barricades of furniture, timber, railings, doors torn from houses nearby, and anything that would help to bar the path of the hated fascists. This magnificent mass action, including and representing all shades of working-class opinion and organisations, Labour, Communist Party, ILP, Trotskyist, League of Youth and Youth Communist League (YCL) – forced the then Commissioner of Police, Sir Philip Game, to order Mosley and his thugs to abandon the route. United action of the workers had defeated Mosley!

The defeat at Cable Street in 1936 dealt a severe blow to Mosley. Afraid of the organised might of the working class so militantly demonstrated, the East End fascist movement declined. The spectacle of the workers in action gave the fascists reason to pause. It induced widespread despondency and demoralisation in their ranks; their victory over the fascists imbued the working class with confidence. This united action of the workers at Cable Street demonstrated anew the lesson: only vigorous counter-action hinders the growth of the menace of fascism.

At that time the Communist Party was mainly responsible for calling militant workers to counter-demonstrations against the fascists. The YCL played a magnificent role. But after 1936 this militant policy of the Communist Party changed and they now avoided any counter-action against the fascists on the wide and militant scale witnessed before. With the coming of Hitler to power the Communist Parties throughout the world had degenerated into nothing but instruments of Russian foreign policy, and their activities reflected this. When Stalin found it impossible to arrive at an agreement with Hitler at that time there was a right about-turn on the part of the then Communist International.

From a refusal to offer a united front with the social democratic workers against fascism, the Communist International embarked on a policy of popular frontism. In line with Stalin's efforts to make agreements and gain alliances with the "democratic" capitalist classes, they advocated class-collaboration between the workers and the "good" capitalists. This foreign policy of the Stalinists was reflected in the British Communist Party which even went to the extent of advocating a "National government" of Churchill, Attlee and Sinclair[47]. Having branded the united front of workers' parties against fascism as "counter-revolutionary", the Stalinists now rejected the Marxist class analysis of capitalist society and advocated a united front with Tories and Liberals.

In their efforts to placate those Tories and Liberals who favoured an alliance with Stalin, the Communist Party made every endeavour to paint itself as just another party of respectable and law-abiding citizens. To that end the hammer and sickle emblem of working-class unity was withdrawn from the masthead of the *Daily Worker*; the language of Marxism was replaced by that of middle-class suburbia. More importantly, the policy of militant class struggle went by the board and this was reflected in the new "ostrich" attitude towards the fascist movement. To take militant action against the fascists would offend the new-found Tory and Liberal "friends" of the Stalinist party. The activities and provocations of the fascists now went unheeded; counter-demonstrations and actions of the workers against fascism were no longer organised. The former policy of militant action was replaced by appeals and pleadings to the state to take measures against the fascists. From a reliance upon the working class to deal with fascism, the Stalinists turned towards a policy of relying on the very state apparatus which had in the so-recent past demonstrated its partiality towards the blackshirts!

How this new policy of the Stalinist leaders worked in practice was indicated by one instance of many similar examples that could be given. Just prior to the war, a monster rally of blackshirts, imported from all over the country into London for the purpose, gathered at Earl's Court to hear Mosley. On that day the Young Communist League of London organised a ramble in the countryside!

Demonstrating against the blackshirt rally outside Earl's Court were only the Trotskyists and a small number of anti-fascist militants. Of the Communist Party there was no sign. This new policy of the Stalinist party served to foster apathy in the ranks of the working class in the struggle against the fascists and emboldened and encouraged

---

[47] Leaders of the Conservative, Labour and Liberal parties respectively.

the blackshirts. It seemed that the fascist movement would gain new strength in face of the lack of organised and militant action on the part of the workers' organisations. But the war cut across these developments and gave them a new direction.

Mosley's "Programme"

Today, in Britain, the signs of a fascist revival are unmistakable. Having tested the reaction of public opinion to the emergence of the various fascist groups, aided and encouraged by police protection, Mosley has launched his new party, the "Union Movement". The new party is no different from the former BUF, the same Jew-baiting, the same promises of the destruction of the trade unions and labour organisations, the same demagogy to attract the disillusioned and despairing middle classes and backward elements.

All Mosley's publications uphold the principle of private enterprise. In one of the recent Mosley "News Letters", he demagogically champions the "small" man, not against the capitalist monopolies, but against the nationalisation measures of the Labour government. Mosley boasts that his "opinions remain unchanged". In his Greater Britain (published before the war) he wrote that: "the making of profit will not only be permitted but encouraged". In an Open Letter to Business Men published in the *Fascist Week*, in 1934, Mosley reassured the industrialists that: "In the corporate state you will be left in possession of your businesses. To the coupon-clipping parasites who live on their dividends, Mosley promised: "Hitherto, the holder of ordinary shares, who is the true risk-bearer in industrial enterprise, has been treated for taxation purposes as the holder of "unearned income"...the whole procedure is illogical, and calculated to discourage the enterprise upon which our industrial future depends."

Whereas before, Mosley emphasised the idea that Britain and the Empire must isolate itself for economic "autarky", today he advocates the "union of Western Europe". Recognising the weakness of British capitalism and the danger of economic collapse on the continent of Europe, Mosley proposes the idea of a union of capitalist Europe based upon the enslavement and exploitation of the African peoples. In the Mosley "plan" "there will be no nonsense about 'trusteeship for the natives'," and "negroes are to have no parity with their white superiors".

One of Mosley's main planks is for war on Russia. If he were in power he would "send Russia an ultimatum that she must accept the American offer to scrap atomic weapons and submit to inspection", which, if unaccepted, would be followed by a "preventive" war.

In the press interview which Mosley gave on 28 November 1947, to announce the imminent launching of his new party, he further elaborated on his "programme". The present parliament would be replaced by the corporate state modelled on Mussolini's two chambers. Instead of elections there would be plebiscites where the voters would have the privilege of recording "yes" or "no" to whatever Mosley's government did. His government would "resign" if defeated, but this, of course, "was most unlikely". Mosley promises to suppress communism.

By this Mosley means that his government would suppress all working-class parties and organisations. The trade unions would be "obsolete" if they did not "cooperate" with the fascists.

The new party of Mosley is thus openly modelled on the fascist totalitarian regimes of Hitler and Mussolini.

Mosley has clearly revealed his calculations. He anticipates being called to power at a time of crisis in the same way as Mussolini was called to power by the Italian monarchy and the Italian capitalists. In his Greater Britain, Mosley wrote:

"If the situation develops rapidly, then the public mind develops slowly, something like collapse may come before any new movement has captured parliamentary power. In that case, other and sterner measures must be adopted for the saving of the state in a situation approaching anarchy. Such a situation will be none of our seeking. In no case shall we resort to violence against the Crown; but only against the forces of anarchy if, and when, the machinery of state has been allowed to drift into powerlessness...

"Anyone who argues that in such a situation the normal instruments of government, such as police and army, can be used effectively, has studied neither the European history of his own time nor the realities of the present situation. In the highly technical struggle for the modern state in crisis, only the technical organisations of fascism and communism have ever prevailed, or in the nature of the case, can prevail. Governments and parties which have relied on the normal instruments of government (which are not constituted for such purposes) have fallen easy and ignoble victims to the force of anarchy. If, therefore, such a situation arises in Britain, we shall prepare to meet the anarchy of communism with the organised force of fascism; but we do not seek that struggle, and for the sake of the nation, we desire to avert it. Only when we see the feeble surrender to menacing problems, the fatuous optimism which again and again has been disproved, the spineless drift towards disaster, do we feel it necessary to organise for such a contingency..."

Thus, the fascists viewed the coming struggle with the forces of "anarchy", i.e. the working class, as an extra-parliamentary one. In the second edition of Greater Britain, Mosley deleted the chapters dealing with this problem, for they were too outspoken. Nevertheless, this remains the basis of Mosley's ideas today. Not accidentally did he declare at the meeting launching the new party on 7 February 1948 that he and his followers were "prepared to meet force with force".

The anti-semitic and anti-working class activities of the fascists are on the increase and although small at present they constitute a challenge to the working class. Fascism must be defeated in its beginnings. The death camps of the nazis, in which hundreds of thousands of German workers were tortured and murdered, should act as a permanent reminder to the working class never to allow themselves to be lulled into a false sense of security. The British fascist movement will not differ from the German or Italian fascists either in social composition, objectives or methods.

The Labour Government and the Fascist Revival

The re-emergence of Mosley and his new "Union Movement" in Britain today is regarded with complacency on the part of the labour leaders. The bitter lessons of Germany and Italy have passed these labour leaders by. They translate into English the same false words and ideas of the German and Italian social-democratic leaders: "It can't happen here." The British, they claim, are "different", a "tolerant" people with a democratic tradition. Fascism is "alien" to the British and so on. Famous last words! The crime of the labour leaders is not that they lull themselves with the pretence that "it can't happen here" but they disarm the working class by sowing illusions and objectively aid the growth of the reviving fascist movement by affording them police protection.

The working class who voted Labour into power may well stand bewildered and indignant as they witness Mosley and the fascists holding provocative meetings under the protection of large numbers of police specially detailed for the job, when they witness the Labour-controlled London County Council affording facilities for Mosley and his movement to meet in schools and halls under their control. This at a time when the fascists have the utmost difficulty in booking public halls because of the pressure of public opinion. Arising out of protests Home Secretary Chuter Ede replied that he is "considering" the banning of loudspeaker equipment at public meetings. But this would apply to "all" parties who use loudspeakers at meetings. This, instead of striking a blow at the fascist movement, in practice would be a blow against working-class organisations who use such equipment for propaganda. This is the result of the "impartiality" of the reformists. Their "impartiality" consists in hamstringing the anti-fascists and allowing the fascists to carry on.

Despite the past six years of terrible war, allegedly to destroy fascism, at the present time, as if nothing had taken place the fascists have taken up from where they left off at the outbreak of the war. The familiar picture of police and courts taking strong action against anti-fascists while the fascists are treated lightly and even protected is once again presented.

All this, in the name of the liberal idea of "democracy", of "impartiality" and "freedom for all". In reality, this is the opposite of freedom as taught by the great socialist teachers. Under this guise of "freedom" and "impartiality" of the state the labour leaders used the police to baton pickets striking for their elementary democratic rights of trade-union organisation. No socialist worker who is not a traitor to his class will put on the same plane the freedom of a scab to break a strike and the freedom of the strikers to prevent him doing so. Yet this force of most despicable scabs, the fascist movement, is given every facility to flourish and prepare to destroy the very right to strike and every other freedom dearly won by the working class. This is neither freedom nor democracy. It is a violation of workers' democracy and the very negation of freedom.

As a crowning piece of folly the labour leaders have given facilities to Mosley to publish his propaganda.

Instead of welcoming the instinctive protests on the part of the workers against any attempted revival of fascist activity, the Labour government organises the police force to protect the fascists against the workers. Labour leaders worthy of the name would welcome workers' action against the reaction and would back it by legislative enactments. This would be a warning to the capitalists that any attempt to establish a fascist dictatorship would be ruthlessly acted on by the labour movement as a whole. In the name of "free speech" the fascists are given every facility to put forward their propaganda, this to the very people who stand for the destruction of free speech and every vestige of democracy won by the working class. In time of war – and the class struggle is a war between the classes – the enemy is not given points of vantage by means of which he can better attack and massacre your own ranks at a later stage.

The election of the majority Labour government after the second world war expressed the aspirations of the British workers to establish a new social system. The masses swung left and in this swing drew behind them large sections of the middle class, whose position had been undermined during the war. The war had placed heavy burdens upon the backs of sections of the middle class, the rise in the cost of living having affected those with fixed incomes most severely. Large numbers of small shopkeepers have been driven out of business by the competition of the big capitalist combines and the measures of concentration encouraged by the state in the interests of "more efficient" big business. Of a total number of 10,000 firms in certain trades in London alone during the war, including furriers, dry cleaners, repairers etc there was a cut of about 40 per cent. As a consequence, the middle class looked to the Labour Party for a solution.

A Gallup Poll revealed that, in the first months of the rule of the Labour government, their popularity increased enormously as a result of the social reforms they introduced. Had the labour leaders introduced wide measures aimed at destroying the privileges and vested interests of the capitalist class, had they taken over all large scale industrial and financial enterprises without compensation and operated the economic life of Britain on the basis of an overall economic plan under the democratic control of the working class, there could have been little effective resistance from the capitalist class. This would have been the socialist solution to the ills which capitalism inflicts not only upon the working class but the middle class as well.

But what is the reality today? Under the Labour government capitalism remains intact. Lavish compensation is given to the previous owners of nationalised industries, which continue to be run on purely "business lines" and largely by the same capitalist managers who were in control before. The overwhelming sector of the economy remains under the control of private enterprise and the nationalised sectors are geared to and serve the interests of private ownership.

Even in the nationalised industries there is not a trace of genuine democratic control by the workers. While the labour leaders talk a great deal about the sacredness of democracy, there is no democratic control extended to the miners or the workers in the industries which are supposedly owned by "the people".

In Britain elements of workers' democracy exist in the form of the trade unions, the workers' parties, factory organisations and the rights which they have won. But the effective control is in the hands of the capitalist class. They control the economic life of the country through their ownership of the means of production; they have the decisive means of influencing public opinion through the control of the press, radio, cinema, schools and church and all other instruments necessary for the purpose. This is the reality of capitalist democracy. Bourgeois democracy, said Trotsky, means that everyone has the right to say what he likes as long as finance capital decides what is done. But once the workers reach out to take real democratic control, then the capitalists decide that the time has come to abolish democracy altogether.

If the labour leaders' chief concern was democracy, they would have introduced real workers' control and democracy. The elements of democracy which are already there would have been brought to full fruition.

Real democracy for the majority and not for the capitalist few, that is, workers' democracy, would mean not only the complete destruction of the economic stranglehold of big business, but the ending of their control of the means of influencing public opinion through their economic control. The Labour government should have immediately taken the press, cinema and radio out of the hands of monopoly capital and placed them at the disposal of the people. Every workers' tendency would be given the fullest free access to the means of propaganda to advocate their point of view. All political parties, including even the Tories and Liberals, who are willing to accept the democratic will of the majority, would have freedom of speech and press. But the fascists would be suppressed outright.

Having organised soviets or workers' committees in the plants and districts and established for the first time a democratic participation of all strata of the population in governing and running the country, the superiority of such a workers' state would be so obvious that any counter-revolution on the part of the capitalist class would be rendered impotent.

Instead of a revolutionary socialist solution, Labour leaders are tinkering with capitalism. The half-and-half measures of the Labour government have resulted in a swing away from Labour, particularly among the middle class and more backward sections of the workers. In the municipal elections of 1947 and in the parliamentary elections of the same year, there was a marked increase in the Tory vote.

And as a symptom of the rightward trend, the fascists re-entered the political arena.

This has taken place in a period of full employment and capitalist boom. British capitalism has lost the advantages she possessed in the past. Despite the efforts of the working class which have resulted in a 20 per cent increase in production over pre-war, there has not been a proportionate increase in the standard of living. Britain is far more dependent on the world market than in the past. With increasing competition the standards of life will not be raised but, on the contrary, the capitalist class will be forced to cut wages.

Already, the Labour government is waging an offensive to persuade the workers to accept a freezing of wages as the exhaustion of the sellers' market looms in sight. With the vociferous applause of the capitalist class and its press, the Labour leaders are exhorting the workers to make more sacrifices in the frenzied drive to increase production and accept a wage freeze and speed-up in the interests of reducing costs in the competitive struggle for world trade.

Cripps explains to the workers that if they do not voluntarily accept the yoke of capital, the British workers will he faced with the iron yoke of totalitarian dictatorship. In his own words:

"It is, therefore, essential that we should get a general agreement amongst our people to act upon sound economic lines: the alternative is likely to prove to he some form of totalitarian government."

The proposals on "sound economic" lines advocated by the labour leaders are, of course, sound capitalist lines.

Here are the symptoms of decline, of impending economic slump, of over-production. Even if the labour leaders should succeed in their objective of increasing production to further record heights, this cannot solve the problem. On the contrary, it can only prepare catastrophe for the Labour government and the British working class.

Under the impact of the radicalisation in 1945, the capitalists were compelled to retreat. But they have not been overthrown by the Labour government. Today they are biding their time. But they are systematically whipping up the discontent of the middle class and backward sections of the workers in preparation for an offensive in the future.

Under the capitalist system, with the crisis of over-production, slump will follow boom as night follows day. And if already the middle class are discontented, how will they react when the slump comes? The workers will be impelled in a revolutionary direction but unless they show the Marxist road, the middle class will be drawn into the orbit of the fascist movement. The capitalists will declare the "Marxists" and the labour movement responsible for the crisis of their system and gain the support of the middle class for action against the workers.

In the grip of economic crisis, the capitalist class will be forced to launch savage attacks on the standards of the workers. They will find the pressure of the workers' organisations irksome, especially the trade unions. Mosley's programme of annihilation of the trade unions and workers' organisations, his defence of private property, arc designed to appcal to big business precisely in such a crisis. To eliminate the unions and terrorise the workers into submission, the capitalists will need fascist bands and will look towards a totalitarian state as the means of their salvation. Then they will really commence to subsidise Mosley or some other fascist less discredited among the population.

There could be no greater danger today than to sit back and content ourselves with the idea that the fascists have little political weight in Britain. While capitalist society exists, the weapon of fascism also exists as a potential menace to the working class. Events may prove that Mosley's "Union Movement" will not be the leading fascist movement in this country. Mosley and his followers were greatly discredited during the war. Nevertheless, some new form of fascist organisation can well arise, an organisation not overtly fascist but of a character similar to de Gaulle's "Rally of the French People" movement which, while it disavows fascism, is, in fundamental policy and aims, designed to serve the same purpose.

As a germ of the disease already present even today in Britain, WJ Brown, Independent MP for Rugby, formerly a leader of Mosley's "New Party" in 1931, has tentatively advocated a "Rally of the British People". Even more indicative is the fact that *the Statist*, in an article Can Our System be Modified?, on 29 November 1947, writes approvingly on General de Gaulle and says:

"General de Gaulle, naturally alarmed by the chaotic state of politics and economics as exemplified in France at present, has asked the people to give him power to form what he calls a national rally. At the same time he warns us that our system is so unstable that it may lead us at a date not indefinitely remote to serious trouble. It should not he wise to ignore such a warning."

Unless the working class can offer some alternative in the form of a bold programme and above all, daring action, the misguided middle-class youth who today support Toryism will be drawn into a fascist movement, whether it be a "Union Movement" or some sort of "Rally of the British People", or "British Royalist Empire Saviours Society".

The Policy of the Communist Party

The revival of fascist activity caused militant workers to look to the Communist Party for a lead. They have been bitterly disappointed. With the exception of a few opposition meetings at Ridley Road in the early days, the Communist Party leadership has undertaken nothing more militant than the organising of Towns meetings under the auspices of the National Council for Civil Liberties, and the passing of resolutions at Trades Councils and Union branches calling upon the Government to take action against the fascists. These joint Towns' meetings include the representatives of the local Labour organisations plus vociferous representatives of local businessmen, Tories and

Liberals. Only the Revolutionary Communist Party has been excluded from the Platforms. This "popular front" with Tories and Liberals is a deception of militant works who seek a fighting policy to defeat the menace of fascism.

To have a united front with Tories and Liberals against fascism is to mis-educate the working class. Instead of teaching them the class nature of fascism, that the capitalist parties represent the very class which will lean on the fascists against the workers, and that only the organised strength of the working class can defeat fascism, they sow illusions and discourage militant action.

The Communist Party recently published an anti-fascist pamphlet entitled *Fascist Threat to Britain*. We advise all workers to read this pamphlet and compare the analysis and the policy with that of the Revolutionary Communist Party. The keynote of the policy of the CP is provided by their description of the war aims of the imperialists. This is what they write:

"Many people took part in this fight. It's no use pretending that the war aims of all the national leaders were exactly the same, or that everyone in the British Army for instance, agreed perfectly. But on one thing every nation and every individual was in complete unity. And that was that the war was being fought to end this thing, fascism, for all time, to crush it without a trace."

History has shown how the "democratic" capitalist class, how the Tory and Liberal spokesmen supported the reaction and fascism abroad. Recent history has shown in World War II that far from being interested in ending this thing fascism, the ruling class merely used the anti-fascist sentiments of the workers for their own imperialist ends. Their attempted deals with Darlan and Badoglio bear witness to the fact that in the very midst of the war, their main concern was to establish regimes capable of dealing with the working class. And in Britain, throughout the so-called war against fascism, the Government refused to publish the "Red Book" of Captain Ramsay, which contained the list of names of fascist supporters in this country.

Yet the Communist Party persists in mis-educating the workers that all nations, all classes were in complete unity during the war in seeking to destroy fascism. Thus the appeal to all sides of political opinion:

"You who are reading this may be a Labour, Liberal, Conservative, or Communist supporter. You may be a trade unionist or co-operator. Whatever your political beliefs we ask you in your own interest, to stand together on this. For if we do not act very soon, democratic discussion and decent living may become impossible."

If we do not act! What action does the Communist Party propose?

"If the fascists come into your locality, get all the inhabitants to sign a petition of protest to the Home Secretary."

But signatures will not frighten fascists.

Following in the footsteps of the ill-fated reformists, the CP confines itself to appeals to the capitalist state machine:

"Demand that existing laws regarding 'incitement to violence' and behaviour 'calculated to cause a breach of the peace' should be strictly enforced: that police should be sent to fascist meetings to make arrests and not to afford protection."

While the CP calls for "vigilance", they urge their members and supporters to stay away from fascist meetings.

Of course, it is necessary to conduct a campaign through the Unions and Labour organisations by means of resolutions, and in order to bring pressure on the Labour Government which claims to speak in the name of the British working class. But what is more essential is that the pressure on the Labour leaders is supplemented by counter-action, by the participation of the workers in combating the fascists. Can anyone deny that the lack of organised counter-action on the part of the workers' organisations has emboldened and encouraged the fascists? Can anyone doubt that had the Communist Party and the YCL in London rallied its powerful organisation and apparatus to counter-demonstrate against the fascists and against Mosley when he first emerged, that they would have thought again before launching their new movement?

The Revolutionary Communist Party has been active in demonstrating and attempting to combat the fascists wherever they have appeared. We wrote to Harry Pollitt appealing for a united front against the fascists. The London District Committee of the RCP sent a similar appeal to the London CP and YCL leaderships. The essence of our position can be summed up in the following extract from the letter sent by the London District Committee to the London District Committee of the Communist Party:

"Despite the very deep and fundamental differences that separate the Trotskyist and the Stalinist Parties at the present time, the London District Committee of the RCP is of the strong conviction that not only is it possible for joint anti-fascist activity between the London members of our respective parties, along practical and specific lines, but that such a united front would meet with enthusiastic support from the rank and file members of our respective organisations. Recent experiences in London have demonstrated that where our comrades have been engaged in anti-fascist activity, a spontaneous united front has been established between members of our organisations with evident success against the fascists."

Our appeals went unheeded at a time when the battles of Ridley Road were at their height and it was imperative that the workers have a united front against the fascists, who were boasting that they had driven the Communist Party from Ridley Road. Instead of rallying to Ridley Road, as the Trotskyists did, the leaders of the Communist Party discouraged their members from gathering there and thus fell into the camp of the petty bourgeois moralists and reformists who said "Ignore them." Despite the cowardly policy of the leadership, many rank and file members of the CP and YCL continued to rally at Ridley Road together with members of the Revolutionary Communist Party and other organisations in a united front of protest. The official line of the CP was far from welcomed by many rank and file militants, whose class instincts correctly led them to participation in the struggle against the fascists.

A revolutionary working class policy must of necessity draw the masses into real participation in the struggle. No amount of appeals for "vigilance" or petitions, resolutions, or appeals to the capitalist state can substitute for the real mass activity of the working class in combating its most dangerous enemies.

How to Fight Fascism – the Policy of the RCP

With the re-emergence of the fascists, the main task of the labour movement is to educate and explain to the workers the class nature of fascism and its function as a combat force against the working-class organisations. But to explain the class roots and function of fascism is not enough. The working class must participate in actively combatting the fascists wherever they raise their heads. For this it is necessary that the organisations of the working class rally the militants around a militant programme of struggle against the anti-semitic, anti-labour propaganda meetings, against the press and other menacing activities of the fascists.

Trade unionists must refuse to print, handle or transport fascist propaganda of any description and demand that their executives make this a rule. All who violate such a rule must be blacklisted.

The first step in mobilising the workers is to unite all sections of the movement – Labour, trade union, Communist Party, Trotskyist, Cooperatives – in a common working-class united front. This is the key to a successful struggle against the menace of fascism. Fundamental differences separate these organisations from each other, but on this question of fascism it is, it must be, possible to have common agreement in forms of struggle. Retaining the right to criticise each other, it is a necessary task to organise joint counter-demonstrations, joint meetings, and joint anti-fascist propaganda campaigns. Fascism is no respecter of working-class opinions and democracy. It seeks to destroy all opposition workers' parties whether they be Labour, Communist, or Revolutionary Communist. To defend and protect working-class meetings and premises, Jewish and other minorities against fascist provocations and attacks, a Workers' Defence Corps must be established based on the trade-union, cultural and political organisations of the working class.

Mosley once boasted that he had a detachment which is joined by "nearly every man who is physically strong...They are highly disciplined in a semi-militaristic manner." Organised detachments of blackshirts can only be combatted by organised detachments of militant proletarians.

In campaigning for the Labour government to "ban the fascists" the workers must bear in mind that history has taught that the enforcement of laws by a capitalist state inevitably acts to the disadvantage of the working class. The state rests upon the army, the police and the courts. And these are riddled from top to bottom with elements sympathetic to the aims of fascism, especially at the top. Even if the pressure of the workers succeeded in enforcing the passage of anti-fascist legislation, clearly it could only be put into effect by the enforcement of the workers. This means that the demand on the Labour government can only be effective when backed by the activities of the organised workers.

This does not mean that we do not strive to bring pressure on the Labour government to take action against the fascists. But it does mean that our demands can only be effective if backed by determined and organised activity on the part of the workers.

We must demand of the Labour government that it immediately:

- Publish the names of all the known pro-fascists contained in the Red Book of Captain Ramsay.
- Publish all evidence and information in the hands of the British Intelligence which reveals the connections between the nazis and the British fascists and representatives of the British ruling class.
- Introduces legislation illegalising the propagation of anti-semitism and race hatred of any form.
- Introduces legislation to make fascist propaganda and organisation illegal and at the same time to protect any section of the population which enforces this law, or is engaged in any activity against the fascists.

Today it is true that the fascist movement is only a small factor in British political life. But from a scratch comes the danger of gangrene! We must not repeat the same mistakes as the German working class.

Historical experience has shown that it is not possible to legislate fascism out of existence. The very nature of the capitalist state precludes that, for fascism in the nature of things is the naked weapon of capitalist class rule. Only the mass of the organised working class, understanding the nature of fascism and with a militant policy of struggle against it, will be capable of dealing effectively with the menace of fascism. In the final analysis the destruction of the capitalist system, which needs and breeds fascism with all its attendant horrors and repressions against the working class and racial and religious minorities, is the only means of ensuring the decisive defeat of fascism.

APPENDIX: Jews in British Society - Some Facts

In its attempt to find a scapegoat for the ills of a disintegrating system, fascism adopts a technique of "Jew-baiting" familiar in the period of feudal decay. All the crimes of monopoly capitalism are blamed on Jewish finance capital. All the discontent of the small shopkeepers and professional men is turned into anti-Semitic channels. Mosley considered this too useful a weapon in the arsenal of his "programme" to let go by.

The fascists attempt to arouse the basest prejudices of the small businessmen and shopkeepers and of backward workers against the Jews. They utilise a deep-rooted superstition dating back to the middle ages that the Jews own, control and manipulate the finances of the country, indeed of the world! Around this banner they do gain support among ignorant people – shopkeepers who meet the competition of Jewish shopkeepers in the same street, or workers who happen to live with Jewish landlords.

Even if it were true that most of the country was owned by Jewish capitalists, this would make little difference to the tasks confronting the working class. It makes little difference to the system whether the capitalists are Jews or Gentiles. Both are subject to the laws of capitalist economy and act accordingly. In a country like Spain where there were no Jewish capitalists (the Jews had been expelled in 1492), poverty, hunger and exploitation of the workers was among the worst in Europe because of the economic circumstances of that country. As is known, the class struggle in Spain culminated in civil war between the workers and the fascists. The Spanish fascists had to find other demagogic slogans. It is interesting to note that De Gaulle is not resorting to anti-Semitism at present.

However, many people, even in the workers' movement give credence to the myth that the Jews control the country. It is necessary for every class conscious worker to know the facts regarding the real position of the Jews in British society, in order to combat the disease. of anti-Semitism.

There are in Great Britain and Northern Ireland only 370,000 Jews out of a total population of 48,000,000. That is, there are 7 Jews to every 1,000 non-Jews, or less than one percent of the population.

The big banks, together with the insurance companies control the country's economy. Yet there is not a single Jew on the Bank of England, either among the Directors or its Executive officials. The Big Five have in all 150 Directors, of these only 4 are Jews.

In international finance, the greatest banking company in the world is J P Morgan & Co. In this company too, there are no Jewish partners and not a single Jew in a leading position.

The Stock Exchange, which dominates the dealings in stocks and shares, and is regarded as a mysterious influence by many small businessmen, is according to the fascists, dominated by Jews. But in fact, on the Stock Exchange Committee there is only one Jew.

Before the nationalisation of the Railways, the number of Directors on the LMS was 18; on the LNER 22; GWR 20; Southern 16; and the LPTB 7. Of these only one was a Jew and one was of Jewish extraction, though his family had been of the Christian faith for several generations.

There are in all 116 daily newspapers and 17 Sunday papers in Britain. Despite the myth that the Jews control the press, there was only one Jew who was director of a newspaper combine; he was Chairman of the Daily Herald but is now dead.

Gaumont British and Odeon Companies were at one time controlled by Jews. They have now passed into the hands of J A Rank, the most powerful figure in the film world, who is in control of some 600 cinemas and practically of all the important studios. The third large corporation, the ABC was never owned by Jews.

Another fascist lie which has gained an ear among some backward sections of the population is that the Jews control the Government and Parliament. In fact there is not a single Jew in the Cabinet. There are only 28 Jewish MPs out of 640. The four Jewish members of the Government are Shinwell, Silkin, George Strauss and Lord Nathan. None is at present in the Cabinet. (A J Cummings, News Chronicle, November 11, 1947)

It is popularly believed that the Jews dominate all black market activities. The facts are that the overwhelming majority of prosecutions both of big and small businessmen for black market offences are not against Jews or people connected with Jewish enterprise. The capitalist press focuses attention on those cases involving Jewish offenders precisely to give the impression that they dominate the black market. Profiteers, whether they be Jews, Gentiles, Irish or Scotch, do not overlook the possibility of extra profit, whether their transactions are legal or not. The whole history of capitalism proves this. The plunder of India, of China and Africa was not carried out by Jews. The slave trade was carried out by religious gentlemen, one of the most notorious of whom named his ship The Jesus!

Of curse, Jews do play a role in business. But in Britain in the decisive industries there is hardly any Jewish capital at all. In iron and steel, engineering, chemicals, automobiles, shipping and rubber, and before nationalisation, coal and railways, Jewish capital is negligible. In the great armaments concerns such as Vickers there is no Jewish capital. However, in certain secondary industries, where the Jews have been traditionally concentrated in different countries, Jewish capital plays an important role. Even here, it is not dominant.

Some facts: In the Tailoring trade one quarter of the total trade is in the hands of Jews, in the Furniture trade one seventh, in Jewellery one fifth, in the Boot and Shoe trade one eighth, two thirds of the Fur trade, but only eleven percent of the Electrical and Radio trade, less than seven percent in Cosmetics. In Food shops one sixth of the trade in London is owned by Jews, but only one sixteenth in the provinces.

In tailoring, Montague Burton's is a Jewish firm. The 50/- Tailors are Gentile. In the bazaar trade, Woolworths, which owns 762 Branches with a capital of £12,000,000 is non-Jewish. Marks and Spencer is a Jewish firm owning 236 Branches with a capital of £3,950,000.

Insofar as chain stores are concerned, the co-operatives, part of the working class movement, is owned by the workers. This is the largest chain store in the country. There are 92 chain store groups with a capital of £150,000 000. The Drapery and allied trade constitute about a third of the capital invested. Half is controlled by non-Jewish firms (Harrods, Selfridges, John Lewis and Barkers). The Unilever Combine which dominates the Groceries and Provisions trade is not, as commonly thought, composed entirely of Jewish capital. The only Jewish capital in this concern is that owned by the Dutch Jews, the Van den Berghs.

On the retail side in the Grocery and Provision trade, Home and Colonial Stores, Maypole Dairies, and even Liptons are not controlled by Jews. The biggest meat combine in the country is the Union Cold Storage which controls 5,000 branches. This is a purely non-Jewish firm. The Jews are totally absent from the Dairy combines: Southern Dairies, United Dairies and Express Dairies are gentile firms. In the Drug trade, the monopoly stores – Boots Taylors, Timothy White's, Savory & Moore's, and Hodders, are all owned by non-Jews.

The decisive section of all industry is controlled by Gentile capital-. The number of small Jewish shopkeepers, retailers, and middlemen, gives a false impression of the role of the Jews in business. In the decisive section of finance the role of Jewish capital is small. Thus, the elimination of the Jews would eliminate none of the injustices of the capitalist system.

The great majority of Jews in Britain, contrary to popular belief, are workers, employed mainly in tailoring, furniture trade, and a fairly high proportion of shop assistants. About 15 percent of the Jews gainfully occupied are in trades and industry on their own account. Of the total population, seven and a half percent are occupied in trade.

The struggle for the emancipation of the working class is not between races or religions. It is one of class against class. Every trace of anti-Semitism, or any form of race hatred cannot assist the oppressed, it can on the contrary only aid the exploiters. Workers of all nationality, religion or creed must stand together against the common enemy: capitalism.

[The facts about the Jews have been collated from *The Jews in Work and Trade* by N. Baron, and published by the Trades Advisory Council, and *Questions and Answers – Facts and Figures of Jewish Economic Life and History*. Publishers as above.]

Fascism and the Workers' Movement
James P. Cannon

1. Notes on American Fascism (A letter to The Militant)

I haven't been able to disentangle myself from other preoccupations to send you any connected thoughts on McCarthyism and the probable character and perspectives of American fascism in general.[48]

The articles of [George] Breitman are very effective arguments against people who will not recognise incipient American fascism until it obliges them by assuming the "classic" European form. What will they do if American fascism neglects or refuses to accommodate them in this respect, right up to the eve of the show down—which it may well do?

I will have something to say about the question of American fascism a little later when I get free from some other commitments. Meantime, I am in basic agreement with the campaign you are conducting and the arguments for it, especially those given in Breitman's articles. I believe these articles would make a good follow-up pamphlet to the first one.

Those who would judge specific American forms of fascism too formalistically by the European pattern, arbitrarily limit capitalist aggression against the workers' movement in two forms:

They see the democratic form by which the workers are suppressed through strictly legal measures in accordance with the law and the Constitution—such as the Taft-Hartley Law, formal indictments and prosecutions for specific violations of existing statutes, etc. All this, despite its obvious "inconvenience" to the workers' movement, is characterised as democratic.

On the other side they see the illegal, unofficial forms of violence practiced by "stormtroopers" and similar shirted hooligans outside the forms of law, as in Italy and Germany. This is characterised as fascist.

But what about violence which is technically illegal and unconstitutional, but carried out nevertheless by duly constituted officials clothed with legal authority? What about such things as the breaking up of meetings and picket lines by official police and special

---

[48] March through April, 1954 in The Militant, New York. James Patrick "Jim" Cannon (February 11, 1890 – August 21, 1974) was the central leader of US Trotskyism until his death in 1974. He was a founder of the Fourth International in 1938, and played a key role in its reunification in 1963.

deputies; wire tapping; inquisitions; screening and blacklisting of "subversives"; and all the rest of the intimidation and terror of the witch-hunt? These procedures don't fit very well into the "democratic" formula, although their chief instruments are legally-constituted officials, supported and incited by press campaigns, radio demagogues etc.

This kind of illegal violence under the outward forms of law has a distinctive American flavour; and it is especially favoured by a section of the ruling class which has very little respect for its own laws, and cares more for practical action than for theories as to how it is to be carried out. This is, in fact, an important element of the specific form which American fascism will take, as has already been indicated quite convincingly.

The depredations of Mayor Hague, who announced that "I am the law", were a manifestation of this tendency back in the late thirties. Trotsky, by the way, considered Hague an American fascist. He described his unconstitutional assaults on free speech and free assembly, through the medium of official police , as a manifestation of incipient American fascism. I think he was right about that. If the workers stand around and wait until the labour movement is attacked directly by unofficial shirted hooligans, before they recognise the approach of American fascism, they may find their organisations broken up "legally" while they are waiting.

The truth of the matter is that American fascism, in its own specific form , has already a considerable army of storm troopers at its disposal in the persons of lawless prosecuting attorneys and official policemen who don't give a damn what the Constitution says. Incipient American fascism—already, right now—has a press and radio-television power which makes Hitler's Angriff look like a throwaway sheet. It has political demagogues, like McCarthy, who are different from Hitler mainly in the fact that they are clothed with official legal powers and immunity, while Hitler had to build up an independent, unofficial and at times persecuted movement without any direct support from the established press, etc.

"McCarthy is different", say the formalistic wiseacres, as if that were a help and a consolation. He is indeed different in several ways. But the most important difference is that he starts with a great power behind him, and operates with formal legal sanction and immunity. The right comparison to make is not of the McCarthy of today with Hitter on the verge of taking power in 1932, but rather with Hitler in the middle twenties. The main difference we find in this comparison is that McCarthy is way ahead of Hitler.

Another point: the German-American Bund of the thirties was not a characteristic manifestation of American fascism, but rather a foreign agency of Hitler's German movement. Neither is it correct to look now for the appearance of genuine American fascism in lunatic fringe outfits such as the Silver Shirts, Gerald Smith, etc. A powerful section of the American bourgeoisie, with unlimited means at their disposal are already fascist-minded ; and they have a big foot in the government, national and local. They feel no need at present of unofficial movements.

To the extent that such outfits will appear here or there, with the development of the social crisis, they will probably be subsumed in a broader, more powerful, adequately financed and press-supported general movement, which operates under more or less legal forms. It is far more correct, far more realistic, to see the incipient stage of American fascism in the conglomeration of "official" marauders represented by McCarthy than outside it.

2. Perspectives of American Fascism

The campaign of the Socialist Workers Party against the ominous upsurge of McCarthyism, and its characterisation of the McCarthy movement as American fascism in incipient form, has been misunderstood by some people who don't want to think, as well as by others who prefer to misunderstand us in order to misrepresent us.

Up till now we have not heard any cogent arguments against our campaign and its motivation. The most we can make out so far are some mutters and murmurs of dissent, to which we will give a preliminary answer while our critics and opponents are getting up the nerve to speak more distinctly.

One of the these muted criticisms appears in a clouded statement in one of the documents of the Pablo faction which Joe Hansen is taking apart in serial articles on another page of *The Militant*. Remarking that the Socialist Workers Party has "sounded the alarm on the fascist danger in the United States"—an accusation which cannot be denied—this document represents the campaign as a sign of our "pessimism", a conclusion which at the very best can be characterised only as a misunderstanding.

There is an obvious contradiction in this recognition of our campaign and the conclusion drawn from it. The woods are full of pessimists about the future of America in general, and about the prospects of American fascism in particular, but they are not organising any campaigns. It is not in the nature of pessimists to do anything of that sort. Pessimism is not merely a gloomy view of evils to come, but a capitulatory reconciliation to them in advance. The real pessimists are simply keeping quiet—concerned to prolong their own grub-like existence, and hoping to adapt themselves to whatever comes by acquiescence and conformity.

The attitude of the SWP is the opposite of all that. The character of a party is not indicated by what it sees and points out but rather by what it does about it. To accuse the SWP of "sounding the alarm on the fascist danger in the US" is only to pay to the party the indirect and unintended compliment of saying that it calls for a struggle against the danger. Pessimists don't sound any alarms or organise any struggles. They just run for cover. Pessimist is just another name for quitter and capitulator.

Some other critical murmurs we have heard, which have not yet found their way into print, represent our campaign as an "exaggeration" of the fascist danger and an apprehension of its imminent victory. That is another misunderstanding. To sound the alarm against the danger of fascism in the United States—and to state frankly that its victory is possible—is by no means to be taken as an admission that fascism is already in power, or close to it. Neither is it to be taken as a prophecy that fascism is destined to conquer eventually.

That will be decided in the struggle. The aim of our campaign is to "alarm" the labour movement to the reality of the danger and, from that, to the necessity of organising the struggle on the right basis while there is yet time. The workers still have time to organise the countermovement, but they don't have forever; and the sooner they recognise the central reality of the whole problem—that the issue will be decided in struggle—the better chance they will have to be the victors.

A fascist movement does not arise from the bad will of malicious demagogues. Neither is a radicalised labour movement created by the propaganda of revolutionists. Both are products of the incurable crisis of capitalism, which renders it unable to maintain a stable rule through the old bourgeois democratic forms. One way or another—these forms will be changed. The latent crisis, which has been artificially suppressed and disguised by war and military expenditures, promises to break out with redoubled fury in the coming period. This will spell impoverishment and misery for tens of millions of people, and it will generate an enormous discontent with the hopeless state of affairs. The unfailing result will be a widespread desire for a radical change.

This mass discontent and desire for a change can take one of two forms, or both of them at the same time.

The workers are the strongest power in modern society. If they show a resolute will to take hold of the situation and effect the necessary revolutionary change, the millions of desperate middle-class people—impoverished farmers, bankrupt small businessmen and white-collar elements—who have no independent power of their own, will follow the workers and support them in their struggle for power. This was demonstrated in the Russian Revolution of November 1917.

On the other hand, if the workers, as a result of inadequate or pusillanimous leadership, falter before their historical task, the allegiance of the middle-classes will rapidly shift to the support of the fascists and lift them into power. This alternative outcome of the social crisis was demonstrated in Italy and Germany.

How will things go in this country? The most "optimistic" way to answer that question is to tell the truth and to say once again: It will be decided in a struggle. Experience of other countries has already shown that a fascist movement and a movement of labour radicalisation, which arise in the first place from the same cause, make their appearance at approximately the same time. But they don't develop at the same rate of speed. The "subjective" factor, the factor of leadership, plays a big role here.

In Italy, and later in Germany, the movement of labour radicalisation had a big jump on fascism at the start. In these two countries fascism began to become a mass movement and a formidable power only after the workers had failed to carry through their revolution when they had the chance—in 1919-1921 in Italy, and in Germany from 1918 to 1923. The tumultuous rise of the fascist movement in those two cases, and its eventual victory, were the answer to the workers' default and the penalty for it.

Here in the United States we see a somewhat different development of the two antagonistic forces—fascism and workers' radicalisation—and a different rate of speed in their development. But these are only tentative manifestations which are not yet by any means decisive. The extraordinary thick-headedness of the labour bureaucracy in this country, and the lack of a revolutionary party with a base of mass support, have given incipient fascism the jump on the labour movement. A form of preventive fascism, of which McCarthy is indubitably the chief representative, has already got a head start and has widespread ramifications of support, inside the governmental apparatus as well as outside it. To recognise that fact is not to conjure up imaginary dangers but simply to recognise the obvious reality of the situation.

And this recognition of reality is the first prerequisite for the organisation of an effective countermovement. McCarthyism, as it appears today, is undoubtedly an incipient fascist movement, but that's all it is. The beginnings of a fascist movement aiming to take power in this country, and fascism already in power, are not the same thing. Between the one and the other lies a protracted period of struggle in which the issue will be finally decided. Whoever recognises that and "sounds the alarm", and thus helps to prepare the struggle of the workers is doing what most needs to be done at the present time. Such a campaign is by no means a manifestation of pessimism, but the best antidote for it.

Power is on the side of the workers, and all the chances of victory are in their favour. But they will never gain the victory without the most resolute struggle. The first prerequisite for that is an understanding of the irreconcilable nature of the struggle and what it's all about. The fate of America, and thereby of all mankind—that's what it's all about.

3. First Principles In The Struggle Against Fascism

The honourable Joseph McCarthy is not much of a thinker himself, but he has certainly stimulated a lot of thought, or what passes for it, in the minds of others. His unbridled aggressiveness in recent months has stirred up quite a fluttering in the dovecotes of so-called liberalism. The pontifical pundits, who yesterday thought the spectre could be exorcised by ridicule, or by pretending not to notice it, are now deep-thinking second thoughts about the Wisconsin demagogue and what he stands for.

Some apprehension of the deadly seriousness of McCarthyism has even begun to dawn in the thick skulls of the official labour leaders, and that alone is testimony to its penetrating power. It is now widely recognised that if the Wisconsin demagogue is crazy, he is crazy like a fox, and has to be taken seriously. It would also seem that the liberals, and the labour leaders who farm out their thinking to the liberals, are catching up with the SWP, as far as the definition of McCarthyism is concerned. Lately we see more and more references to McCarthy as an American Hitler. For example, Adlai Stevenson, who cannot justly be called an extremist, referred to McCarthy in his Miami speech as the apostle of a "malign totalitarianism".

But we are still poles apart from the liberals and the labour skates on the main question, that is, the analysis of the causes of this preliminary manifestation of a "malign totalitarianism"—the Stevensonian euphemism for fascism—and the program for struggle against it. They all regard our revolutionary approach to the question as extreme and unrealistic. The unrealism, however, is on their side, because they separate McCarthyism from the social causes which have generated it, and which in fact, make such manifestations inevitable. If McCarthy did not exist American capitalism would have to invent him, or a reasonable facsimile.

In every great social struggle, those who understand its laws and foresee how it must develop according to those laws, have a big advantage over those who deal with surface manifestations. If the Socialist Workers Party had been the first and only group in American political life to state categorically that the rise of a fascist movement in the United States is an absolute certainty., and likewise the first to recognise McCarthyism as the preliminary manifestation of American fascism, and to call it by its right name—this was not guesswork in either case.

Our approach to the question of American fascism, as to every other political issue, begins with and proceeds from a basic theory of American perspectives which is different from that of all other political parties and tendencies. That is not because we deny America's exceptional position in the world today. It is known, and has been said often enough, that American capitalism is in a different position from other sectors of the same world in other countries. I am even willing to repeat it once again if such reassurance will do anybody any good. But there are points of similarity as well as of difference, and the former are more important than the latter. That is the main point.

The American capitalists are richer and stronger than their counterparts in other lands. They are also younger and more ignorant, and therefore more inclined to seek a rough settlement of difficulties without diplomatic subtlety and finesse. All that does not change the fact that American capitalism operates according to the same laws as the others, is confronted with the same fundamental problems, and is headed toward the same catastrophe.

Of all the mistakes that can be made in judging the nature and prospects of the present social system in this country—and it is safe to predict that the American labour leaders, being what they are, will exhaust every possibility in this respect—the worst and most disorienting mistake is to regard American capitalism as fundamentally different; as immune from the operation of the same laws which determine the evolution and development of the same social system—through crisis, revolution and counter-revolution—in other countries.

This pernicious theory of "American exceptionalism", which seized the leadership of the American Communist Party in the latter days of the great boom of the twenties, disoriented the party in the great crisis which exploded soon afterward. This same theory, which is today held by the entire labour officialdom, is what disarms the American workers at the present time more than anything else, and gives the preliminary movement of American fascism such an easy advantage in the beginning.

We Trotskyists never belonged to this school of "exceptionalism". In 1946, right at the time when the editorial spokesmen of American capitalism were proclaiming the advent of the "American Century", and the American labour leaders were adjusting their so-called thinking to this illusory prospect, the Socialist Workers Party outlined a different and more realistic perspective for this country. The "Theses on the American Revolution", adopted by the party convention in that year, expressed its conception in the very first paragraph, as follows:

The United States, the most powerful capitalist country in history, is a component part of the world capitalist system and is subject to the same general laws. It suffers from the same incurable diseases and is destined to share the same fate. The overwhelming preponderance of American imperialism does not exempt it from the decay of world capitalism, but, on the contrary, acts to involve it ever more deeply, inextricably and hopelessly. US capitalism can no more escape from the revolutionary consequences of world capitalist decay than the older European capitalist powers. The blind alley in which world capitalism has arrived, and the US with it, excludes a new organic era of capitalist stabilisation. The dominant world position of American imperialism now accentuates and aggravates the death agony of capitalism as a whole.

This formulation of American perspectives, which governs all the work of the party, determines its analysis of McCarthyism as the incipient stage of American fascism; its categorical assertion that this movement will grow bigger, stronger and more cohesive with the development of the oncoming crisis; and its program for the struggle against it.

Some such manifestation as the present McCarthy movement was foreseen; and it needed only to make its appearance and score some initial successes, as it has manifestly done since the Brownell-Truman affair, for the party to react with its counter-campaign of agitation. The fact that the party members have recognised the necessity of the campaign, and responded to it with unanimous participation, is a sign that they were prepared for it by a long previous period of doctrinal education.

I speak of our view of American fascism as a doctrine; for we consider it a matter of principle that the war prosperity of US capitalism has been sick with a latent crisis from the start: and that this crisis is bound, sooner or later, to explode with devastating fury. This exploding crisis is certain to produce two antagonistic phenomena, a fascist movement on the one side, and a radicalised labour movement on the other.

The same social crisis which poses the threat of revolution in each and every capitalist country without exception, likewise generates the attempt to head off such a revolution by means which ruthlessly break down all the old forms of democratic rule. An organised fascist movement is an imperative necessity to the ruling class in every modern capitalist state threatened with social revolution, and is, in fact, a reflexive answer to it. In this view, the fascist movement is not something arbitrarily created by demagogues, to be talked down by appeal to reason and an alliance of all men of good will. Fascism is organised counter-revolution.

There is no law which forbids such a counter-revolutionary movement to get under way before the prospect and threat of revolution is clearly evident to all. A social revolution is immanent in the present position of American capitalism, and so is the counter-revolution. McCarthyism, as the first definite preliminary manifestation of the counter-revolutionary movement, does not lose this basic characteristic simply because it is a preventive mobilisation against a revolution which has not yet taken visible form.

McCarthyite fascism has its cause and origin in the crisis of a social system which is pregnant with a revolution; and is in fact, the preliminary form of a preventive counter-revolution. A general hue and cry against McCarthyism won't amount to much until this is recognised.

4. A New Declaration Of Independence

Fascism is a product of the crisis of capitalism and can be definitively disposed of only by a solution of this crisis. The fascist movement can make advances or be pushed back at one time or another in the course of this crisis; but it will always be there, in latent or active form, as long as the social causes which produce it have not been eradicated.

Looked at from this standpoint, the threat of American fascism is not a short-term problem, and by no means can it be eliminated at the next election—or, for that matter, at any other election. The American fascist movement, and the workers' struggle against it, will be a long drawn-out affair, from now to the final showdown, which in the end can be nothing less than a show down between fascist capitalism and the workers' revolution.

If the default of the labour movement has given American fascism, in the incipient and preventive form represented by the McCarthy movement, an advantage at the start, it still represents nothing more than an episode in a long struggle which will have many ups and downs. The real movement of American fascism is now only in its preliminary stages of formation, and the countermovement of the workers against it is not even started yet.

At any rate, American fascism, in its McCarthyite form or under some other aegis, is bound to provoke a militant resistance from the workers as soon as it passes over from its present preoccupation with a hunt for spies and "subversives" to a direct assault on the labour movement. Thereafter, the fascist movement will not develop on a straight ascending line. There will be zigzags on one side and the other, advances and set backs and periods of stalemate. In this protracted conflict the labour movement will have time to get a clearer picture of the real nature of the problem, and to mobilise its forces for an all-out struggle.

At the present time, the myopic policy of the liberals and the labour leaders is concentrated on the congressional elections next fall, and the presidential election to follow in 1956. A Democratic victory is counted on to deal a death blow to the McCarthy aberration. "McCarthyism is becoming a danger all right, and it begins to look like a fascist movement; but all we need is a general mobilisation at the polls to put the Democrats back in power." Such are the arguments we already hear from the Democratic high command, the literary liberals, the labour leaders and—skulking in the rear of the caravan, with their tails between their legs—the Stalinists.

This would really be laughable if humour were in place where deadly serious matters are concerned. The Roosevelt New Deal, under far more favourable conditions, couldn't find a way to hold back the economic crisis without a war. A Stevensonian version of the same policy, under worse conditions, could only be expected to fail more miserably. A Democratic victory might arrest the hitherto unobstructed march of McCarthyism while it re-forms its ranks. It might even bring a temporary moderation of the fury of the witch-hunt. But that's all.

The fascist movement would begin to grow again with the growth of the crisis. It would probably take on an even more militant character, if it is pushed out of the administration and compelled to develop as an unofficial movement. Under conditions of a serious crisis, an unofficial fascist movement would grow all the more stormily, to the extent that the labour movement would support the Democratic administration, and depend on it to restrain the fascists by police measures.

Such a policy, as the experience of Italy and Germany has already shown, would only paralyse the active resistance of the workers themselves, while giving the fascist gangs a virtually free rein. Moreover, by remaining tied to the Democratic administration, the labour movement would take upon itself a large part of the responsibility for the economic crisis and feed the flames of fascist demagogy around the question.

That would be something to see: The fascists howling about the crisis, and stirring up the hungry and desperate people with the most extravagant promises, while the labour leaders defend the administration. The official labour leaders are fully capable of such idiocy, as they demonstrated in the last presidential election. But with the best will in the world to help the democratic administration, they couldn't maintain such a position very long.

The workers will most probably accept the recommendation of the labour leaders to seek escape from the crisis by replacing Republican rascals by Democratic scoundrels in the next election. But when the latter become officially responsible for the administration, and prove powerless to cope with the crisis, the workers will certainly draw some conclusions from their unfortunate experiences. The deeper the crisis, and the more brutal the fascist aggression fed by the crisis, the more insistent will be the demand for a radical change of policy and a more adequate leadership.

From all indications, the workers' discontent will be concentrated, at first, in the demand for a labour party of their own. This will most probably be realised. It will not yet signify the victory over fascism— not by a long shot—but it will represent the beginning of a countermovement which will have every chance to end in victory.

The break with the Democratic Party will be an implicit recognition that the fight against fascism is fundamentally a fight against capitalism in the period of its agonising crisis of disintegration and decay; and that there is no hope of victory for the workers in alliance with one of the parties of this same capitalism, and still less under its leadership, as at present. The formation of a labour party, based on the trade unions, will represent the American workers' Declaration of Independence. It will be a great turning point in American history. All developments will be speeded up after that.

It would be a great mistake, however, to speak of a prospective labour party as the solution of the problem of fascism. As in 1776, the new Declaration of Independence will signify not the end, but the beginning of the real struggle. The final outcome will depend on the program and the leadership. These will become the burning issues of an internal struggle for which the labour party will provide the main arena. It is from this point of view—clearly stated at all times—that we advocate the formation of a labour party and do all we can to hasten the day of its appearance.

5. Fascism And The Labour Party

Our campaign against McCarthyite fascism is an agitational campaign to arouse the labour movement to the advancing danger, and to stimulate a countermobilisation of the workers. Along this road we participate wholeheartedly in every practical action regardless of its official auspices. Such actions have a logic of their own and can lead, in a step-by-step process, to a final settlement of accounts with fascism and the social system which turns to fascism as a last resort.

The struggle against fascism is an affair of the working class, and the revolutionists would only defeat their own purpose by sectarian abstention from antifascist mobilisation of the class. *The Militant* is certainly correct in calling for a general congress of labour, to consider the question of a united antifascist struggle of the entire labour movement; and in advancing the slogan of a labour party as the general formula for the political independence of the workers in this struggle..

But even while advancing and popularising these slogans, which sooner or later will be accepted and supported by millions, we ought to explain their limitations as well as their advantages. The assertion that the labour party "will stop McCarthyism", which makes its way into our agitation now and then, is an oversimplification which ought to be guarded against. A labour party would represent a gigantic step forward in the struggle against fascism, but is not in itself a panacea for victory.

A fascist movement is an inherent necessity to the capitalist system at a given stage of its disintegration. Nothing will "stop fascism" short of the overthrow of capitalism. This is the simple truth of the matter, and if our party doesn't tell this truth constantly it would have no reason to exist. There are plenty of others to sow confusion and foster illusions, and they are not entitled to any direct or indirect help from us. There is good ground for confidence that the workers will prevail in the final showdown, and that fascism will never come to power in America. But there is no ground for the assumption that the workers' victory will be quick and easy, or that a mere demonstration of organised labour's opposition would scare the fascist menace off the map.

The workers of Germany were politically organised in two great mass parties. Moreover, the communist and social-democratic parties of Germany, who shared the allegiance of almost the entire working class between them, were at least formally committed to a socialist program. They collapsed under the blows of fascism just the same, precisely because they hoped for the miracle of victory without a real struggle. That would surely happen in this country too, even with a labour party supported by the entire trade-union movement, if it should offer no more resistance to fascism than plaintive objections and parliamentary opposition.

I believe it is correct to say that a real first step toward a serious struggle against American fascism could hardly be anything less than the formation of a labour party. As long as the trade unions are allied to the Democratic Party and thereby, in effect, dependent on capitalist politicians to protect them against the onslaughts of a fascist party dedicated to a capitalist counter-revolution—they have not even begun to fight.

For that reason, it is perfectly correct to put the slogan of a labour party in the centre of our agitation and to concentrate all agitation around it. But in doing so, we have no need to oversimplify the fundamental problems posed by the beginnings of a fascist movement, and to think that we are doing our full duty if we stop at that. We must look far ahead—from the beginning of the struggle to the end—and keep the goal in mind in all that we do and say. We have to be with the workers in all their practical actions and in all their struggles. But we will be no help to them if we simply follow along, keep quiet about the workers' present illusions and thereby foster them.

If we see the impending struggle in its true shape as a drawnout affair, we must recognise that coming developments will work powerfully to realise the slogans of the present. After that, new events will prepare the conditions for a widespread acceptance of the more advanced slogans required at a later stage of development. As a revolutionary party, we ought to foresee these developments and formulate the necessary slogans in advance.

Looking to the future, as measured now only in years rather than in decades or generations, it can be expected that a labour party will take shape and command the allegiance of millions of workers from the start. This will represent a real beginning of the antifascist mobilisation of the American working class, which will just be another name for the mobilisation against capitalism, of which fascism is the final resort. But our agitation, and our participation in practical actions leading to this preliminary mobilisation, will have real importance and significance only to the extent that we keep the whole line of future developments in mind and prepare ourselves and others to meet them.

If the slogan of a labour party based on the trade unions is the most correct and necessary general slogan of agitation at the present time, the simultaneous explanation of the inescapable trend of developments toward a revolutionary showdown, and the building of a party of conscious revolutionists based on this perspective, cannot be put aside in the meantime. The two tasks go together; and taken together, they constitute the most important work of preparation for things to come.

6. Implications Of The Labour Party

The formal launching of an Independent Labour Party, the indicated next step in the preliminary mobilisation of the American working class against a rising fascist movement, will hit this country like a bomb exploding in all directions. It will not only blow up the traditional two-party system in this country and bring about a basic realignment in the general field of American politics. It will also mark the beginning of a great shake-up in the labour movement itself. The second result will be no less important than the first, and it should be counted on.

Under the present system the political stage is occupied by two rival capitalist parties, which in reality represent two different factions of the ruling class. The workers play merely the part of a chorus in the wings and have no speaking part on the stage. The formation of a labour party will change all that at one stroke. The struggle of capitalist factions for control of the government will be subordinated to the struggle of classes, represented by class parties. That is the real meaning of politics anyway.

The political realignment, brought about by the appearance of a labour party on the scene, cannot fail to have profound repercussions inside the labour movement. There will be a great change there too. The break of the trade-union movement with capitalist politics will coincide with the rise of the big opposition to the present official leadership. This rank-and-file opposition movement will most likely take shape in the struggle for a labour party, and be identified with it.

To imagine that the present official leaders can make the great shift from the Democratic Party to independent labour politics, and maintain their leadership smoothly in an entirely new and different situation, requires one to overlook the basic causes which will force them to make this shift. That is, the radicalisation of the rank and file and their revolt against the old policy. No matter how it is formally brought about, a labour party will be the product of a radical upsurge in the ranks of the trade unionists. The more the officialdom resists the great change, the stronger will grow the sentiment for a different leadership. Even if the present leaders sponsor the labour party at the start, they will be under strong criticism for their tardiness. The real movement for a labour party, which will come from below, will begin to throw up an alternative leadership in the course of its development.

The demand for a labour party implies the demand for a more adequate leadership., and the actual formation of a labour party, under the auspices of the present official leadership, would only accelerate the struggle under more favourable conditions. As revolutionists, we advocate the formation of a labour party with this perspective also in mind.

It is true that the simple fact of the formation of a labour party, by itself, would have a profound influence in speeding up radical and even revolutionary developments. But those who are satisfied with that might as well retire from the field and let the automatic process take care of everything. The automatic process will not take care of anything except to guarantee defeats. The conscious revolutionists, however few their numbers may be in the beginning, are a part of the process. Their part is to help the process along by telling the whole truth. The fight for a labour party is bound up with the fight to cleanse the labour movement of a crooked and treacherous leadership, and cannot be separated from it. Those radicals and ex-radicals who are willing to settle for a labour party, leaving the question of program and leadership unmentioned, are simply inventing a formula for their own betrayal.

It is not permissible for revolutionists to pass themselves off as mere advocates of a labour party, pure and simple, like any labour faker who devotes Sunday sermons to this idea. A labour party headed by the present official labour skates, without a program of class struggle, would be a sitting duck for American fascism. That's the truth of the matter, and advocacy of a labour party isn't worth much if it leaves this truth unsaid. Large numbers of trade-union militants know this as well as we do. They know that the present official leaders are no good for a real fight on any front, and that they have to be thrown out before there can be any serious thought of a show down with American fascism.

Those militants who know the score on this ought to organise themselves in order to conduct their struggle more effectively. This organisation of the class conscious workers can only take the form of a revolutionary party. There is no substitute for that. And since the SWP is the only revolutionary party in the field, there is no substitute for the SWP. Those workers who today already recognise the necessity of a labour party ought to take the next step and unite with the SWP in its effort to direct the struggle toward a revolutionary goal.

Counter-mobilization to Racism & Fascism
Farrell Dobbs

The current outbreak of rightist movements—Youth for Goldwater, John Birch Society, the extremist American Nazis, etc.—requires close attention and it also poses some tactical questions that need clarification.[49]

Implicit in this trend is the ultimate danger of repressive fascist attacks on labour and its allies, against which the labour movement will have to wage a showdown struggle in the streets. But it would be a serious mistake to raise a hue and cry against incipient fascism, as though the ultimate danger were already upon us, and attempt to substitute ourselves for the masses in taking the issue to the streets here and now. National politics still remains class collaborationist in mass character, despite the growing restiveness of labour and its allies. While this class political equilibrium remains operative, fascism can't make significant headway. When the present equilibrium does become upset through a labour breakaway from capitalist politics, it does not necessarily follow that capitalism will resort forthwith to fascist measures. An attempt might be made, as class political antagonism sharpen, to establish bonapartist rule, perhaps through a military dictatorship based on the present vast interlocking alliance between the officer corps and the monopoly capitalists. Fascist trends would receive strong new impulses at such a conjuncture, but the ultimate showdown with fascism would still not be at hand. Therefore our propaganda, in addition to explaining the meaning of fascism and educating the masses in the need to be on guard against it, must also analyze the complex interim questions of the power struggles which could be next on the agenda.

At the present time, given the class collaborationist character of national politics, the existing rightist formations simply represent vanguard polarizations on the right which play the counterpart of our vanguard role on the left. They can do little more than conduct propaganda, resorting only to isolated, small scale acts of hooliganism which often backfire against them. Since the incipient fascists are not strong enough to carry through antidemocratic actions at present, a

---

[49] Political Report to the June 1961 SWP Convention (excerpt). Reprinted from SWP Discussion Bulletin, Vol. 22, No. 19, September 1961. Farrell Dobbs (1907 –1983) was a US Trotskyist and trade unionist. From 1948 to 1960 he was the SWP's candidate for President of the United States and succeeded James P. Cannon as national secretary of the party in 1953.

call for mobilization against them would give the general impression of an attempt on our part to suppress freedom of speech and assembly for others. We would not only be inviting comparable attacks, both legal and extra-legal, against our own democratic rights, but we would appear to have given them justification. The truth is that we stand for freedom of speech and assembly in principle—not just for us, but for everybody. Therefore, we do not demand that the rightist movements be denied these freedoms.

Concerning the question of civil liberties, we should keep in mind that our growing reputation as a serious revolutionary tendency with a meaningful program is drawing attention not only from people becoming radicalized. The witch hunters are taking notice as well. We are beginning to draw their fire to a new degree in connection with the Cuban defence movement and there could be other new attacks. More than ever we must be on guard against any undermining of civil liberties for all, if we hope to defend our own democratic rights. To act otherwise would be to repeat the costly mistake of the Stalinists in refusing to recognize the democratic rights of their political opponents.

Let me call to your attention an article Trotsky wrote on this subject in December 1939 in the *Socialist Appeal* under the title, "Why I Consented to Appear Before The Dies Committee." I don't have the time to give you the background but it's worth your while to go back and do a little research on the circumstances surrounding the question of Trotsky possibly testifying before the Dies Committee, intending to use the occasion for propaganda purposes.

The questions of Stalinist dictatorship, of democratic rights under capitalism and the policy of revolutionists on civil liberties in a capitalist country like ours came up in this discussion. Trotsky wrote in the article cited, "Being an irreconcilable opponent not only of fascism but also of the present-day Comintern, I am at the same time decidedly against the suppression of either of them." He pointed out that the suppression of fascists by the capitalist government always proves fictitious. He also took note of the fact that to defend the rights of the Stalinists could help to refurbish the Comintern. "However," he said, "the question is not exhausted by this consideration. Under the conditions of the bourgeois regime, all suppression of political rights and freedom, no matter whom they are directed against in the beginning, in the end inevitably bear down upon the working class, particularly its most advanced elements. That is a law of history."

In the article Trotsky was speaking of a specific stage, the one we're in now, where we're struggling under adverse conditions against a repressive ruling class in a capitalist country. He pointed out that when the struggle intensifies into a class showdown a new factor arises, the rules of civil war, which are something else again. But concerning a situation such as ours, he stated unambiguously "the working class in the capitalist countries, threatened with their own enslavement must stand in defence of freedom for all political tendencies including their own irreconcilable enemies."

Under circumstances where the foregoing policy will be maintained, we may at times find it useful propagandistically to organize counter-demonstrations against incipient fascists. In any situation where they resort to rightist hooliganism we will take the initiative in organizing defence guards to oppose them. But our central task at this stage concerning the rightist formations is to explain the true nature of fascism in our propaganda, seeking to educate and alert the masses against it. In doing so we must keep a sense of proportion as to the immediate nature of the fascist issue, being careful to direct major attention to the primary questions of the day.

Notebooks for Study and Research

- 1 The Place of Marxism in History, Ernest Mandel   (40 pp. €5.)
- 2 The Chinese Revolution - I: The Second Chinese Revolution & the Shaping of the Maoist Outlook, Pierre Rousset   (32 pp. €5)
- 3 The Chinese Revolution - II: The Maoist Project Tested in the Struggle for Power, Pierre Rousset   (48 pp. € 5)
- 4 Revolutionary Strategy Today, Daniel Bensaïd   (36 pp. €5)
- 5 Class Struggle and Technological Innovation in Japan since 1945, Muto Ichiyo   (48 pp. €5)
- 6 Populism in Latin America, Adolfo Gilly, Helena Hirata, Carlos M. Vilas, and the Partido Revolucionario de los Trabajadores (Argentina) introduced by Michael Löwy   (40 pp. €5)
- 7/8 Market, Plan and Democracy: The Experience of the So-Called Socialist Countries, Catherine Samary   (64pp. €5)
- 9 The Formative Years of the Fourth International (1933-1938), Daniel Bensaïd   (48 pp. €5)
- 10 Marxism & Liberation Theology, Michael Löwy   (40pp € 5)
- 11/12 The Bourgeois Revolutions, Robert Lochhead   (72pp. €5)
- 13 The Spanish Civil War in Euzkadi and Catalonia 1936-39, Miguel Romero   (48pp. €5)
- 14 The Gulf War and the New World Order, André Gunder Frank and Salah Jaber   (72pp. €5)
- 15 From the PCI to the PDS, Livio Maitan   (48pp. €5)
- 16 Do the Workers have a Country?, José Iriarte "Bikila"   (48pp. €5)
- 17/18 October 1917: Coup d'état or Social Revolution, Ernest Mandel   (64pp. €5)
- 19/20 The Fragmentation of Yugoslavia: An Overview, Catherine Samary   (60pp. €5)
- 21 Factory Commitees and Workers' Control in Petrograd in 1917, David Mandel   (48pp. €5)
- 22 Women's Lives in the New Global Economy, Penelope Duggan & Heather Dashner (editors)   (68 pp. € 5)
- 23 Lean Production: Capitalist Utopia? Tony Smith   (68 pp. €5)
- 24/25 World Bank/IMF/WTO: The Free-Market Fiasco, Susan George, Michel Chossudovsky et al.   Out of print
- 26 The Trade-Union Left and the Birth of a New South Africa, Claude Jacquin   (92 pp., €5)

- 27/28 Fatherland or Mother Earth? Essays on the National Question , Michael Löwy (108 pp., €16, £10.99, $16)
- 29/30 Understanding the Nazi Genocide: Marxism after Auschwitz, Enzo Traverso (154 pp., €19.20, £13, $19.)
- 31/32 Globalization: Neoliberal Challenge, Radical Responses, Robert Went (170 pp., €21, £14, $21)
- 33/34 The Clash of Barbarisms: September 11 & the Making of the New World Disorder, Gilbert Achcar (128 pp., €15, £10, $16)
- 35/36 The Porto Alegre Alternative: Direct Democracy in Action, Iain Bruce ed. (162 pp., €19, £13, $23.50)
- 37/38 Take the Power to Change the World, Phil Hearse ed. (144 pp., €9, £6, $12)
- 39/40 Socialists and the Capitalist Recession (with Ernest Mandel's 'Basic Theories of Karl Marx') Raphie De Santos, Michel Husson, Claudio Katz (196 pp., €9, £7, $12)
- 41 Living our Internationalism: The IIRE's history, Murray Smith and Joost Kircz eds. (104pp, €5, £4, $7)
- 42/43 Strategies of Resistance & 'Who Are the Trotskyists' Daniel Bensaïd (196 pp. €8, £6, $10)
- 44/45 Building Unity Against Fascism: Classic Marxist Writings, Leon Trotsky, Daniel Guérin, Ted Grant (164 pp., €8, £6, $10)
- 46 October Readings: The development of the concept of Permanent Revolution, D. R. O'Connor Lysaght ed. (110pp, €5)
- 47 The Long March of the Trotskyists: A contribution to the history of the International, Pierre Frank (168 pp €8, £6, $10)
- 48 Women Liberation & Socialist Revolution: Documents of the Fourth International, Penelope Duggan ed. (194pp €8, £6, $10)

Forthcoming

- Dangerous relationships, Marriage and divorces between Marxism and feminism, Cinzia Arruzza
- Marxism and Anarchism, Marx, Lenin, Trotsky et al.
- New Left Parties: Experiences from Europe, Bertil Videt et al.
- Returns of Marxism, Sara Farris and Antonio Carmona Báez eds.
- Revolution and Counter-revolution in Europe, Pierre Frank
- The conflict in Palestine, Cinzia Nachira ed.
- Women and the Crisis, Terry Conway ed.

Subscribe online at: http://bit.ly/NSRsub
To order, email iire@iire.org or write to International Institute for Research and Education, Lombokstraat 40, NL-1094, Amsterdam.

www.ingramcontent.com/pod-product-compliance
Lightning Source LLC
Chambersburg PA
CBHW032043040426
42334CB00038B/551